ASIAN POLITICAL, ECONOMIC AND SECURITY ISSUES

EFFECTS OF U.S.-KOREA FREE TRADE AGREEMENT ON SMALL AND MEDIUM-SIZED ENTERPRISES

ASIAN POLITICAL, ECONOMIC AND SECURITY ISSUES

Additional books in this series can be found on Nova's website under the Series tab.

Additional E-books in this series can be found on Nova's website under the E-book tab.

TRADE ISSUES, POLICIES AND LAWS

Additional books in this series can be found on Nova's website under the Series tab.

Additional E-books in this series can be found on Nova's website under the E-book tab.

ASIAN POLITICAL, ECONOMIC AND SECURITY ISSUES

EFFECTS OF U.S.-KOREA FREE TRADE AGREEMENT ON SMALL AND MEDIUM-SIZED ENTERPRISES

BRIAN M. SULLIVAN
EDITOR

Novinka

New York

For permission to use material from this book please contact us:
Telephone 631-231-7269; Fax 631-231-8175
Web Site: http://www.novapublishers.com

Library of Congress Cataloging-in-Publication Data

ISBN: 978-1-62808-843-4

Published by Nova Science Publishers, Inc. † New York

Contents

PREFACE

The U.S.-South Korea Free Trade Agreement (KORUS FTA) is the second-largest U.S. FTA (next to NAFTA). South Korea is the seventh largest trading partner of the United States, and the United States is South Korea's third-largest trading partner. The KORUS FTA covers a wide range of trade and investment issues and, therefore, could have substantial economic implications for both the United States and South Korea. KORUS FTA encompasses a range of bilateral economic activities: trade in manufactured goods, agricultural products, and services; foreign investment; government procurement; intellectual property rights; and worker rights and environment protection, among other issues. The United States and South Korea entered into the KORUS FTA as a means to further solidify an already strong economic relationship by reducing barriers to trade and investment between them and to resolve long-standing troublesome economic issues. The United States specifically sought increased access to South Korean markets for agricultural products, services, and foreign investment. For South Korean leaders, the KORUS FTA is a mechanism to promote reform in its own economy and also to gain a competitive advantage in the U.S. market for autos and other manufactured goods. This book examines the provisions of the KORUS FTA in the context of the overall U.S.-South Korean economic relationship, U.S. objectives, and South Korean objectives. It also examines some of the issues that have arisen during its implementation.

Chapter 1 - With the entry into force of the U.S.-Korea Free Trade Agreement (FTA) on March 15, 2012, a very large share of U.S. exports of consumer and industrial products were eligible for duty-free entry into the Republic of Korea (Korea), as the number of Korea's tariff lines providing immediate duty-free access for U.S. exports increased from 13 percent to 80 percent. In addition, the FTA increases market access commitments in major services sectors and includes provisions for addressing nontariff measures as well as trade-related issues such as labor, environment, and competition policy. This report examines the FTA's effects on exports by U.S. small and medium-sized enterprises (SMEs), which account for a significant share of U.S. exports both in general and to Korea. To provide information for the report, SMEs were queried about their experiences thus far in exporting to Korea under the FTA. A small number of companies provided the requested information, with responses coming from firms in diverse sectors of the economy, including agriculture (wine, tree fruit, potatoes, hay), manufacturing (tool and die, aircraft parts), and services (media, software).

Responding SMEs reported varying experiences. Several indicated immediate sales increases, while others reported that potential trade gains have been delayed because of long implementation time frames. Narratives of expanding business opportunities and the creation of new relationships were partly countered by concerns about remaining nontariff measures (such as current phytosanitary restrictions) and new administrative burdens. Nonetheless, most respondents expressed the belief that the FTA had already proven helpful and would benefit their companies even more over time.

Chapter 2 – On October 3, 2011, President Obama submitted draft legislation (H.R. 3080/S. 1642) to implement the U.S.-South Korea Free Trade Agreement (KORUS FTA) to both houses of Congress. On October 6, the House Ways and Means Committee reported out H.R. 3080 (H.Rept. 112-239). The Senate Finance Committee reported out S. 1642 (without written report). On October 12, the House passed H.R. 3080 (278-151) and sent it to the Senate which passed it (83- 15). The President signed the legislation on October 21, 2011 (P.L. 112-41). In South Korea, after a contentious battle, the Korean National Assembly passed the agreement on November 22. On March 15, 2012, the KORUS FTA entered into force.

The KORUS FTA is the second-largest U.S. FTA (next to NAFTA). South Korea is the seventh-largest trading partner of the United States, and the United States is South Korea's third-largest trading partner. The KORUS FTA covers a wide range of trade and investment issues and, therefore, could have substantial economic implications for both the United States and South Korea.

Congress approved the KORUS FTA implementing legislation using expedited procedures authorized by the Trade Promotion Authority (TPA). Under TPA, the President had the discretion on when to submit the implementing legislation to Congress. The KORUS FTA was negotiated and signed on June 30, 2007, by President George W. Bush. However, President

Bush did not submit the legislation because of differences with the Democratic leadership over treatment of autos and beef, among other issues. On December 3, 2010, after a series of arduous negotiations, President Obama and President Lee announced that they had reached an agreement on addressing the outstanding issues related to the KORUS FTA. As a result, U.S. and South Korean negotiators agreed, in the form of an exchange of letters and agreed minutes, to modifications to the commitments made in the 2007 agreement. These modifications included changes in phase-out periods for tariffs on autos and pork, a new safeguard provision on autos, and concessions by South Korea on allowing a larger number of U.S. cars into South Korea under U.S. safety standards than was the case under the original KORUS FTA provisions. The modifications were included in the implementing legislation.

A broad swath of the U.S. business community supported the KORUS FTA. With the modifications in the commitments reached in December 2010, this group also included the three Detroit-based auto manufacturers and the United Auto Workers (UAW) union. It still faced opposition from some labor unions and other groups, including Public Citizen. Many U.S. supporters view the KORUS FTA as important to secure new opportunities in the South Korean market, while opponents claimed that the KORUS FTA does not go far enough to break down South Korean trade barriers or that the agreement will encourage U.S. companies to move their production offshore at the expense of U.S. workers. Other observers suggested the KORUS FTA could have implications for the U.S.-South Korean alliance as a whole, as well as on U.S. Asia policy and U.S. trade policy.

In: Effects of U.S.-Korea Free Trade Agreement … ISBN: 978-1-62808-843-4
Editor: Brian M. Sullivan

Chapter 1

U.S.-KOREA FREE TRADE AGREEMENT: EFFECTS ON U.S. SMALL AND MEDIUM-SIZED ENTERPRISES*

United States International Trade Commission

ACRONYMS

A2IM	American Association of Independent Music
AAMSI	Associated Aircraft Manufacturing and Sales Inc.
c.i.f.	Customs, insurance, and freight
CPA	Coalition for a Prosperous America
EU	European Union
FMVSS	Federal motor vehicle safety standards
FTA	Free trade agreement
GDP	Gross domestic product
IMF	International Monetary Fund
IP	Intellectual property
MEMA	Motor & Equipment Manufacturers Association
MFN	Most favored nation
mt	Metric tons
NAFTA	North American Free Trade Agreement

* This is an edited, reformatted and augmented version of United States International Trade Commission, Investigation No. 332-539; USITC Publication 4393,dated May 2013.

NHC	Northwest Horticulture Council
OEM	Original equipment manufacturer
SME	Small and medium-sized enterprise
TRQ	Tariff-rate quota
USITC	United States International Trade Commission
USTR	United States Trade Representative

EXECUTIVE SUMMARY

With the entry into force of the U.S.-Korea Free Trade Agreement (FTA) on March 15, 2012, a very large share of U.S. exports of consumer and industrial products were eligible for duty-free entry into the Republic of Korea (Korea), as the number of Korea's tariff lines providing immediate duty-free access for U.S. exports increased from 13 percent to 80 percent. In addition, the FTA increases market access commitments in major services sectors and includes provisions for addressing nontariff measures as well as trade-related issues such as labor, environment, and competition policy. This report examines the FTA's effects on exports by U.S. small and medium-sized enterprises (SMEs), which account for a significant share of U.S. exports both in general and to Korea. To provide information for the report, SMEs were queried about their experiences thus far in exporting to Korea under the FTA. A small number of companies provided the requested information, with responses coming from firms in diverse sectors of the economy, including agriculture (wine, tree fruit, potatoes, hay), manufacturing (tool and die, aircraft parts), and services (media, software).

Responding SMEs reported varying experiences. Several indicated immediate sales increases, while others reported that potential trade gains have been delayed because of long implementation time frames. Narratives of expanding business opportunities and the creation of new relationships were partly countered by concerns about remaining nontariff measures (such as current phytosanitary restrictions) and new administrative burdens. Nonetheless, most respondents expressed the belief that the FTA had already proven helpful and would benefit their companies even more over time.

SECTION 1. INTRODUCTION

Purpose and Background

This report by the United States International Trade Commission (USITC or Commission) discusses the effects of the U.S.-Korea Free Trade Agreement (FTA) on the production, distribution, and export strategies of U.S. small and medium-sized enterprises (SMEs). It describes how U.S. SMEs have benefited from specific provisions of the FTA and details the challenges that SMEs still face in exporting to the Republic of Korea (Korea) since the FTA's entry into force. This report contains information collected by the Commission from SMEs about their experiences before and after the FTA's entry into force and their expectations regarding the FTA's effect on their firms. This report was prepared at the request of the United States Trade Representative (USTR) in a letter dated January 29, 2013, with a requested report delivery date of May 1, 2013.[1]

With the entry into force of the FTA on March 15, 2012, a very large share of U.S. exports of consumer and industrial products were eligible for duty-free entry into Korea, as the number of Korea's tariff lines providing immediate duty-free access for U.S. exports increased from 13 percent to 80 percent.[2] Besides cutting tariffs, the FTA increases market access commitments in major services sectors and includes provisions for addressing nontariff measures as well as trade-related issues such as labor, environment, and competition policy.[3] On the date of entry into force, Korea and the United States also established a Working Group on SMEs to address issues affecting SMEs during implementation of the FTA. The USTR requested this report to assist the work of the Working Group on SMEs, which is expected to meet later in 2013.

Some of the information in this report was taken from a series of three Commission reports from 2010 on the role and importance of SMEs in U.S. exports generally.[4] As an indication of the importance of exports in general and the Korean market specifically to U.S. SMEs, the Commission found in the first report that SMEs accounted for 30.2 percent of U.S. merchandise exports in 2007 and that Korea was the seventh-largest market for U.S. exports by SMEs in 2007 (the most recent year for which such data were available).[5]

Scope

The scope of this report encompasses all sectors of the U.S. economy as defined by the North American Industry Classification System. Similarly, the U.S. merchandise export data used in this report encompass all Sections of the international Harmonized Commodity Description and Coding System. Comparable data for U.S. exports of services to Korea were unavailable.

The definitions of "enterprise" and "SME" are the same as those used in the USITC reports referenced above. This report uses the U.S. Census Bureau (Census) definition of an enterprise, which is a business organization consisting of one or more domestic establishments under common ownership or control. For the purposes of this report, the terms "enterprise," "firm," "business," and "company" are used interchangeably. "SMEs" refers to enterprises with less than 500 employees in the agriculture, manufacturing, and service sectors.[6]

Although the FTA entered into force on March 15, 2012, the basic agreement was signed in 2007, giving SMEs an opportunity to plan and adjust their strategies to take advantage of reductions in duties and other trade impediments once the FTA entered into force. In light of that lead time, the Commission sought information about plans made before and after the FTA entered into force.

Information Sources

In keeping with the focus of this report on the FTA's effects as identified by the SMEs themselves, this report consolidates the information provided through telephone and in-person interviews of SME representatives conducted by Commission staff and through written submissions made by SMEs, supplemented with information from the SMEs' websites. [7] The Commission generally did not seek to corroborate or verify the information and views received. Primary background data are derived from Census figures. The Commission invited interested persons to file written submissions for this investigation. Those submissions are available at the Commission's Electronic Docket Information System (https://edis.usitc.gov/edis3-internal/app).

To identify companies that are SMEs, that have exported or possibly would export to Korea, and that might have insight into the effects of the FTA on their production, distribution, and export strategy, Commission staff contacted business and industry associations, consulted industry and trade literature, distributed notices via the foreign and domestic networks of other U.S. government agencies, and searched public and proprietary databases. Through interviews, direct mail, third-party distribution, and other methods, Commission staff attempted to contact an estimated 4,000-plus potential study participants, and a small number of companies provided the requested information. The Commission also received five written submissions, which are summarized in Appendix B.

Organization of the Report

Section 2 presents an overview of the state of the Korean economy in the periods before and after the entry into force of the FTA, as well as data on the patterns of U.S. exports to Korea during those periods. Section 3 summarizes the information obtained by the Commission from SMEs and other sources about the effects of the FTA on the production, distribution, and export strategy of U.S. SMEs since the FTA entered into force; how U.S. SMEs may have benefited from specific provisions of the FTA; and challenges they have faced in exporting to Korea. Appendix A contains a copy of the USTR's request letter. Appendix B summarizes the positions of interested parties who submitted written statements to the Commission in connection with this investigation.

SECTION 2. KOREAN ECONOMIC CONDITIONS AND U.S. EXPORTS

This Section gives an overview of the state of the Korean economy during 2007–12 and of U.S. exports to Korea during the 24-month period ending in February 2013 in order to help compare the bilateral trade environment facing U.S. SMEs in the year before and the year after the FTA's entry into force. Because trade statistics on U.S. SME exports for 2011–13 are not currently available, this Section uses data on total U.S. merchandise exports to Korea from March 2011 through February 2013, the latest month for which these data are available. In particular, it compares data from March 2012 through February 2013—the period the FTA has been in force—with data from the same months in 2011–12.

The Commission found that since the FTA's entry into force, U.S. exports to Korea have risen in certain sectors, although total U.S. exports to Korea have declined. However, because of the short time frame and the presence of external factors (briefly discussed below), among other aspects, this Section does not seek to analyze the FTA's effects.

The Korean Economy

The Korean economy was projected to be the world's 15th largest in 2012.[1] Korea was the fifth-largest global exporter that year, following the European Union (EU), China, the United States, and Japan, with total goods exports of $548 billion and a trade surplus of $28.3 billion. In 2012, Korea was also the fifth-largest global importer, after the EU, the United States, China, and Japan, with goods imports of $519.6 billion.[2] Imports from the United States accounted for 8.3 percent of total Korean imports in the full year 2012, down from 8.5 percent in the full year 2011, making the United States Korea's fourth-largest import partner after China, Japan, and the EU.[3]

In 2011, which was the latest year for which international data on trade in services are available, Korea ranked 10th in total services imports and 12th in total services exports.[4]

Korea was the 11th-largest destination for U.S. services exports in 2011.[5]

Real growth in Korea's gross domestic product (GDP) slowed in 2011 and 2012, on the heels of strong growth in 2010 (figure 2.1). Korea's position as a significant participant in global trade makes the country's economy sensitive to swings in demand for its exports. In 2012, weak growth in global demand for Korean exports contributed to a slowdown in Korean production.[6] The intensifying European sovereign debt crisis in 2011 and 2012 lowered demand for Korean exports not only in the EU itself, but also in markets such as China and Japan, which import Korean inputs for use in products they export to the EU.[7]

Total Korean exports declined by a small amount, 1.3 percent, in full year 2012 (figure 2.1). Similarly, Korean import levels declined by 0.9 percent in 2012 after three years in which growth exceeded 20 percent annually (figure 2.1).

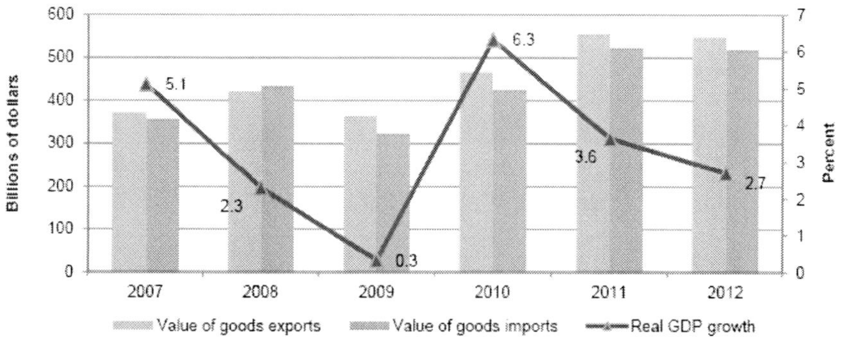

Source: Global Trade Atlas database; IMF International Financial Statistics, World Economic Outlook (October 2012).

Figure 2.1. Korean real GDP growth (right axis) and goods exports and imports (left axis), 2007–12.

U.S. Exports to Korea

U.S. exports to Korea from March 2012 to February 2013 were worth $39.2 billion, a decline of 7.2 percent from the same period in 2011–12 (table 2.1). By comparison, total Korean imports fell 3.4 percent in value during the same period (table 2.1).

Table 2.1. U.S.-Korea trade, March 2011–February 2012 and March 2012–February 2013

	March 2011–February 2012	March 2012–February 2013	Percent change
	Billion $	Billion $	
U.S. exports to Korea	42.3	39.2	–7.2
Total U.S. exports	1,317.0	1,357.6	3.1
Total Korean imports	534.6	516.5	–3.4

Source: Compiled from official statistics of U.S. Department of Commerce and data from the Global Trade Atlas database.

Although total U.S. exports to Korea declined in the period in which the FTA has been in effect, exports in certain sectors rose. U.S. exports to Korea of beverages and tobacco products, chemicals, textiles, and transportation equipment grew the most strongly during this period (table 2.2). The U.S. sectors suffering the greatest declines in exports provide goods that may be used as inputs to Korean production, including petroleum and coal products manufacturing, plastics and rubber products manufacturing, and fabricated metal product manufacturing.

Table 2.2. U.S. exports to Korea, by industry, March 2011–February 2012 and March 2012–February 2013

NAICS3 sector description	March 2011–February 2012	March 2012–February 2013	Percent change
	Million $	Million $	
Apparel manufacturing	113	98	–13.3
Beverage and tobacco product manufacturing	129	162	25.5
Chemical manufacturing	6,398	6,841	6.9
Computer and electronic product manufacturing	6,179	5,939	–3.9
Electrical equipment, appliance, and component manufacturing	1,084	1,057	–2.5
Fabricated metal product manufacturing	1,404	1,043	–25.7
Food manufacturing	3,019	3,047	0.9
Furniture and related product manufacturing	30	28	–6.5
Leather and allied product manufacturing	164	182	10.8
Machinery manufacturing	5,919	5,437	–8.1
Miscellaneous manufacturing	852	821	–3.7
Nonmetallic mineral product manufacturing	394	394	0.1
Paper manufacturing	505	485	–3.9
Petroleum and coal products manufacturing	915	486	–46.9
Plastics and rubber products manufacturing	355	282	–20.4
Primary metal manufacturing	1,112	1,099	–1.1
Printing and related support activities	77	70	–9.4
Textile mills	49	51	3.9
Textile product mills	78	71	–9.1
Transportation equipment manufacturing	4,502	4,660	3.5
Wood product manufacturing	52	49	-5.6
All nonmanufactured products[a]	8,945	6,939	–22.4
All products	42,273	39,241	–7.2

Source: Compiled from official statistics of U.S. Department of Commerce and official Census statistics.

[a] Includes agricultural and mining commodities, certain publishing services, scrap, and used goods.

U.S. exports of services to Korea from April to December 2012 were $13.3 billion, an increase of 8.4 percent compared to the same period in 2011 (table 2.3). The categories of services exports that experienced the largest increase in the period were royalty and license fees (23.4 percent) and travel (10.0 percent). The other transportation category, which includes freight and port services for goods traveling by ocean or air, saw a decline in sales to Korea of 4.8 percent.

Table 2.3. U.S. exports of services to Korea, by sector, April–December 2011 and April–December 2012

Sector	April–December 2011 (million $)	April–December 2012 (million $)	Percent change
Travel[a]	2,637	2,901	10.0
Passenger fares	106	112	5.7
Other transportation (freight and port services)	1,659	1,580	–4.8
Royalties and license fees	3,494	4,311	23.4
Other private services (education, financial, insurance, telecommunications, computer and information, management and consulting, research and development, leasing, and other business services)	4,256	4,272	0.4
U.S. government miscellaneous services and transfers under			
U.S. military agency sales contracts	151	159	5.3
Total U.S. exports of services to Korea	12,301	13,335	8.4

Source: Bureau of Economic Analysis, U.S. International Transactions.

Note: Data on U.S. exports of services to Korea in the fourth quarter of 2012 are the latest available at the time of publication. Sum of sectors may not add to total due to rounding or reporting inconsistencies.

[a]U.S. exports of travel services consist of expenditures by foreign residents traveling in the United States.

Section 3. U.S. SMEs and Korean Market Experiences

This Section summarizes information provided by U.S. SMEs discussing the effects of the U.S.-Korea FTA on their production, distribution, and export strategies and describing how they have benefited from specific provisions of the agreement, as well as challenges that they may have faced in exporting to

Korea. The information presented is drawn from companies' written and oral statements to the Commission and information taken from company websites. Appearing first are summaries of statements from agricultural SMEs (the majority of respondents), followed by summaries of statements from firms in manufacturing and services.

Agriculture

U.S. agricultural SMEs witnessed some immediate improvements in the trading environment when the FTA entered into force, primarily from lowered or eliminated tariffs and higher quota levels. For example, several U.S. SME exporters of hay and of cherries reported quick sales improvements and the creation of new business relationships as a result of these changes. However, U.S. SME potato exporters who responded stated that they saw no short-term gains and, in fact, faced a new phytosanitary restriction that limited existing sales. SME exporters of cherries and other fruit said that they continued to face Korean phytosanitary restrictions, which the FTA's entry into force did not address. U.S. SME wine producers' comments were mixed: one said it had yet to see any change in its export levels despite the duty elimination, while another reported it was having immediate success, emphasizing its product's new price competitiveness with other foreign wines in the Korean market.

Potatoes

Potato producers' comments addressed three types of issues: tariff reduction, phytosanitary measures (measures intended to protect plant health), and business relationships.

Tariff Reduction

Under the FTA, chip-stock potatoes[1] and table-stock potatoes are treated separately. Chip-stock potato imports from the United States were granted unlimited duty-free access to Korea during a five-month period of the year, while an annual duty-free tariff-rate quota (TRQ) of 3,000 metric tons (mt) was established for U.S. table-stock potatoes.[2]

Allied Potato, a grower, marketer, and exporter primarily of chip-stock potatoes with operations in Washington state and California, had anticipated that the initial reduction in the duty on chip-stock potatoes under the FTA would entice some Korean customers to consider trying U.S. product and that export volumes would increase further as the tariff rate fell over time. The firm reported that it has seen a slow and steady increase in shipments as new trade relationships have been established, and it expects to export higher volumes to Korea next year and in the future.[3]

Phytosanitary Issues

In response to concerns about zebra chip disease,[4] Korea banned all fresh potato imports from Idaho, Oregon, and Washington in August 2012, including table-stock and chip-stock potatoes, but relaxed this restriction for chip-stock potatoes in October 2012. Table-stock potatoes from these three states continue to be banned from the Korean market. Before the restriction, Strebin Farms, a producer and exporter of table-stock and chip-stock potatoes from Oregon, stated that it regularly shipped table-stock potatoes to Korea and, in mid-2012, had already scheduled a shipment. The shipment was canceled due to the new phytosanitary restriction. Strebin Farms stated that because of the imposition of phytosanitary restrictions in the months following implementation of the FTA, gains from the agreement have not yet materialized for the firm; in fact, sales to Korea have actually declined compared to previous years.[5]

Wada Farms, an Idaho grower, shipper, and marketer of table-stock potatoes, said that it has never shipped to Korea, but made efforts to do so after the FTA entered into force. However, the ban on table-stock potatoes was implemented before the company could make any sales, and the firm expressed frustration that a new market opportunity had opened and then closed before it could take advantage of it. The firm stated that it would be interested in exporting to Korea in the future but is unable to do so as long as the phytosanitary restrictions remain in place.[6]

Business Relationships

Allied Potato said that one of the main benefits of the FTA's entry into force has been the creation of an incentive for launching U.S.-Korean business partnerships. The firm reported that it has seen a slow and steady increase in shipments as new trade relationships have been established and the quality of the product has been demonstrated. The company said that it had not previously considered Korea to be a market with large growth potential, but now the firm is reevaluating its overall export strategy and planning to export higher volumes to Korea next year and in the future.[7]

Overall View of the FTA

The three firms all saw the FTA as holding promise for the future, if not for the present.

- Allied Potato stated that while its opinion of the FTA is positive, its expectations of benefits under the agreement have not yet been fully realized because it will take time for the advantages to become apparent.[8]
- Strebin Farms said that the entry into force of the FTA was, at least conceptually, a positive event, but because of the imposition of phytosanitary restrictions the firm's sales to Korea have actually declined compared to previous years. In the long run, the firm is optimistic that U.S. shipments to Korea of table-stock and chip-stock potatoes will grow steadily, but it believes that the phytosanitary dispute must be resolved before the playing field will truly be leveled.[9]
- Wada Farms characterizes the FTA as an "opportunity on hold."[10]

Hay

The hay producer's comments focused on the FTA's effect on access to the Korean market.

Market Access

Of the wide variety of hay and other fodder products, hay in general entered Korea under an annually variable TRQ before the FTA entered into force. The largest category of U.S. hay exports to Korea now enters under a new 200,000 mt duty-free TRQ.[11] Consequently, Anderson Hay & Grain[12] of Washington state, a producer and exporter of hay, said that it benefited from increased market access following the entry into force of the FTA. In addition, under the FTA Korea will phase out tariffs on all U.S. hay and fodder exports by 2026, during which period Anderson Hay projects a steady rise in exports.[13] Anderson Hay reported that it experienced sizable growth in its exports to Korea in 2012 and an increased stability and regularity in its sales and shipment patterns. Further, it increased export sales not only to long-established business partners inside Korea, but also to new companies that sought out U.S. hay and straw supplies once the agreement came into force. The firm expressed strong support for the agreement.[14]

Fruit

Three fruit producers commented on the FTA, expressing their views as to the positive effects of tariff reduction as well as challenges posed by Korean phytosanitary measures.

Tariff Reduction

Under the FTA, Korea immediately eliminated its MFN duty of 24 percent ad valorem on eligible imports of U.S. cherries, and according to the three firms responding in this sector, that elimination has been the primary driver behind increased U.S. cherry exports to Korea. Oneonta Starr Ranch Growers, a Washington grower, packer, and marketer of apples, pears, citrus, cherries, and other stone fruits, said that the elimination of the duty on U.S. cherries has greatly reduced prices at the retail level, bringing new consumers into the market for cherries. The company said that because the tariff was assessed on the customs, insurance, and freight (c.i.f.) value of the goods and cherries are shipped to Korea via air freight, which increases the c.i.f. value dramatically, its impact on the cherries' final retail price was substantial.[15]

Sage Fruit Company, a grower, packer, and marketer of apples, pears,[16] and cherries located in the Yakima Valley of Washington state, stated that before the FTA ended the tariff on cherries, the company had exported only small volumes of cherries to Korea for a limited time. Sage Fruit said that as a result of the tariff elimination, demand for cherries from Korean importers, including many that historically had been customers of Sage Fruit, has risen, and the market now provides higher returns than other markets. Sage Fruit stated that its export volumes to Korea are still small, but it believes they will continue to grow as a result of the tariff elimination.[17]

Stemilt Growers, a grower, packer, and marketer of apples, pears, and cherries in Wenatchee, Washington, stated that since the FTA's entry into force and the immediate tariff elimination, the firm's cherry exports to Korea have almost doubled compared with the same period the previous year. The company reported that the reduction in cost due to tariff elimination was significant enough to attract new middle- and lower-income consumers and increased interest from nontraditional cherry marketers, such as smaller retailers, hotels, and restaurants in second-tier cities. Further, although growth in U.S. exports to Korea over the past year was partially spurred by a large U.S. cherry harvest, the firm expects future growth in exports to Korea to continue at a high rate, possibly between 20 and 30 percent annually.[18]

Phytosanitary Issues

Cherry exporters expressed frustration about the methyl bromide fumigation requirements that Korea imposes on U.S. cherry exports to Korea. Oneonta stated that the fumigation shortens shelf life and forces exporters to ship cherries by air, which is far costlier than sea freight.[19] Sage Fruit explained that years ago, when Japan implemented a systems approach protocol as an alternative to fumigating cherries with methyl bromide, the company stopped shipping cherries to Korea and began shipping to Japan.[20] Without fumigation, the quality of the fruit was higher, increasing demand and resulting in higher prices in the Japanese market.[21]

Concerning apples and pears, Oneonta and Stemhilt Growers said that long-standing Korean phytosanitary issues, which were not addressed by the FTA, continue to restrict full market access for U.S. pear and apple exports.[22] There are currently no U.S. apple or pear exports to Korea for consumption in the Korean market. Stemilt Growers stated it had not necessarily expected the FTA to resolve the issues, but that it is hopeful they may be resolved faster due to the existence of the FTA and the related working group on sanitary and phytosanitary issues.[23]

Overall View of the FTA

All three respondent firms expressed positive opinions of the FTA, although two included caveats.

- Stemilt Growers stated that it views the FTA positively.[24]
- Similarly, Sage Fruit said that it has a positive reaction to the opportunities that the FTA is providing and stated that although the FTA's entry into force has not resulted in the resolution of long-standing phytosanitary issues, such as the methyl bromide fumigation requirement for cherries and the lack of market access for U.S. apples and pears, it hopes that the agreement might provide the political environment and mechanisms to resolve these issues.[25]
- Oneonta also stated that although it hopes these issues can be settled under existing provisions of the FTA, it realizes that resolution of these types of issues tends to be a long, complicated process.[26]

Wine

The two responding wineries expressed differing views on the effect of the FTA's elimination of tariffs on wine from grapes; one also commented on the FTA's positive influence on the development of U.S.-Korea business relationships.

Tariff Reduction

Wine from grapes is now free of duty, compared with the MFN rate of 15 percent ad valorem applied to U.S. exports of wine from grapes before the FTA entered into force. Wente Vineyards in California[27] stated that the tariff elimination and resulting drop in retail prices for wine has lowered the margins between U.S. wine and wine from other countries, specifically Chile and those in Europe,[28] and increased demand for U.S. wine. Wente Vineyards stated that the entry into force of the FTA has resulted in tremendous growth for U.S. wine in the Korean market, with exports increasing by approximately 40 percent. According to Wente Vineyards, although the entire Korean market for wine has been growing rapidly, the growth in its exports and exports of all U.S. wine is now outpacing the growth of most European and South American exporters.[29]

In contrast, Silver Oak, another California winery,[30] stated that the elimination of the 15 percent Korean tariff on U.S. wine as a result of the FTA's entry into force has not had an impact on the company's exports to Korea or on prices of U.S. wine at the retail level in Korea. The company stated, however, that it was not expecting an immediate impact on retail prices from the tariff elimination because price adjustments often take time to filter through the supply chain.[31]

Business Relationships

Wente Vineyards stated that the FTA's entry into force has increased marketing awareness and renewed interest from Korean importers and retailers in U.S. wines. This development has allowed the company to expand the number of retailers that market its product.[32]

Overall View of the FTA

- Wente Vineyards said that it has positive impressions about the agreement and its own growth prospects in the Korean market.[33]
- Although Silver Oak suggested that Korea may be a growth market for its wine exports and U.S. wine exports in general in the future, the firm indicated that the major driver of that growth will likely be different marketing approaches adopted by Korean distributors and importers and not necessarily any specific provisions or effects of the FTA.[34]

Manufacturing

Certain Manufactures and Chemicals

Three U.S. SME manufacturers expressed the view that the U.S.-Korea trading environment has improved since the FTA entered into force, with new business possibilities, a strengthening of existing relationships, and more-regular sales patterns. One mentioned a new administrative requirement, but said that it was a minor burden. Each of these manufacturers said that it had exported to Korea before the FTA's entry into force and anticipates greater opportunities under the FTA.

Tariff Reduction

As a result of the FTA's entry into force, the duty on eligible imports of U.S. steel, copper, and nickel springs was reduced from 8 percent to free. Optimum Spring Solutions, a Florida manufacturer of high-quality custom springs[35] that exported to Korea before the FTA's entry into force, indicated that its products now cost less in Korea, which has helped the company strengthen its ties to Korean customers (see "business relationships"). The company stated that about one-half of its sales are export sales to various markets.[36]

Transpo Industries, a New York company that manufactures and supplies safety products and new-technology materials for bridges, roadways, tunnels, railroads, airports, and ports, exports a product called T-48 to Korea. It is designed to be used principally as a high-resistant top coat applied to bridges and other road surfaces and also as a sealant on existing cracks and other defects in damaged road surfaces. Transpo said that it has exported T-48 to Korea during the past five years; the 6.5 percent duty on T-48 was eliminated when the FTA entered into force.[37]

Business Relationships

AAMSI, a Florida exporter of parts and components for helicopters, military jets, and ships to Korea,[38] stated that it has been exporting more products to Korea since the FTA's entry into force. However, the company did not attribute the rise in its exports to the FTA, given that exports of these parts had been receiving duty-free treatment before the entry into force. The company said that the FTA has created a positive atmosphere for business relations with Korea. AAMSI is projecting further expansion of its business operations in Korea, and the company is studying plans to work with potential Korean partner companies to perform aircraft repair in Korea.[39]

Optimum Spring Solutions said that a customer contact in Korea stated that it has become more convenient to deal with the United States since the FTA entered into force. Optimum Spring Solutions stated that business relationships with Korean customers have become stronger and more stable because its products now cost less in Korea, making the company more competitive in a global context and allowing the company to maintain its level of employment in the United States.[40]

Market Access

Transpo reported easier movement of its product into the Korean market and improved access to the Korean marketplace in general since the FTA's entry into force. The company stated that it is "aggressively" pursuing additional trade opportunities afforded under the provisions of the agreement. For example, Transpo is working to improve the regularity of its sales patterns, which were sporadic before the FTA's entry into force, together with an improvement in export volumes.[41]

Administrative Issues

Optimum Spring Solutions noted that it must now provide a one-page certificate of origin with each shipment to Korea to confirm that its products are made in the United States. However, the company considers this new requirement to be a minor inconvenience in comparison to the important benefits of the FTA.[42]

Services

The three U.S. services SMEs that responded expressed mixed views of the FTA's effects. The two entertainment SMEs viewed the FTA as having a helpful influence on intellectual property (IP) protection, while the third respondent, a software services firm, focused more on administrative concerns and the question of whether its recently improved sales in Korea were tied to the FTA's entry into force.

Music-related Services

Intellectual Property

Two responding SMEs, CMJ Holdings and WBA Entertainment Inc./335 Records, while not citing any provisions in the IP section of the FTA or changes in Korean law per se, reported substantial new opportunities in Korea attributable at least in part to what they regard as the improved IP environment.[43] CMJ Holdings Corp., a New York SME that connects music fans and music industry professionals with new music through interactive media, live events, and print, said that it participated in a trade mission to Korea and other Asian countries in September 2012,[44] and saw direct and indirect benefits from this visit. Shortly after the trade mission, a Korean organization hosted and promoted CMJ at a music conference. And in 2013, for the first time, Korean companies will participate as sponsors in CMJ's annual Music Marathon, a music conference and festival in New York. This participation will mean substantial music-related services spending in the United States by Korean trade associations and firms, as well as spending on other U.S. services such as travel, tourism, and promotional services. CMJ states that the combination of strong IP regulations and low prices for legal access to music has substantially reduced musical piracy in Korea, creating additional value for U.S. artists' work.[45]

WBA Entertainment Inc./335 Records, a professional talent management and production firm in Tennessee whose president is co-founder of the independent music label 335 Records, also participated in the September 2012 trade mission to Asian countries. WBA Entertainment/335 Records noted that IP protection is critical to SMEs in the music industry. Because improved IP protection helps artists control and produce income from their creative work, WBA Entertainment/335 Records generally had a positive view of the FTA's effects.[46]

Software-related Services

While it reported rising sales of its products in Korea, DiSTI—the software firm responding in this category—cited the effect of administrative costs on SMEs in particular.

Administrative Issues

DiSTI, a Florida company that sells software tools and services for the development of visual interfaces used in automotive digital dashboards, medical device interfaces, and aviation display controls,[47] expressed concern over possible administrative costs under the FTA. The firm reported that despite NAFTA, its exports to Canada are almost nonexistent because the general administrative costs have become too great; it stated that such costs alone exceed what it makes in the sale of software and services. DiSTI predicted that if the same types of administrative cost issues arise in Korea, its exports to Korea will decline because smaller companies such as DiSTI usually depend more heavily on on-hand cash flow and revenue streams.[48]

Overall View of the FTA

- DiSTI noted large increases in demand from the Korean automotive sector for its software products and services, although it is unsure if this is a direct result of the FTA's entry into force. Despite its concerns about administrative costs, the firm continues to have a positive outlook and expects to see its market share grow in Korea.[49]

References

Global Trade Information Service Inc. (GTIS). World Trade Atlas database (accessed March 18, 2013).

Ibarra-Caton, Marilyn, and Charu Sharma. "U.S. International Services: Cross-Border Trade in 2011 and Services Supplied through Affiliates in 2010." *Survey of Current Business* 92, no. 10 (October 2012): 15–58.

International Monetary Fund (IMF). *Balance of Payments Statistics: Yearbook 2012*. Washington, DC: IMF, 2012.

———. World Economic Outlook database, October 2012. http://www.imf.org/external/pubs/ft/weo/2012/02/weodata/index.aspx.

Kim, Cynthia. "Korea Output Unexpectedly Falls As Europe Caps Demand." Bloomberg, July 30, 2012. http://www.bloomberg.com/news/2012-07-30/south-korea-industrial-production-falls-as-europehurts-exports.html.

Suszkiw, Jan. "Bacterium Identified as Prime Suspect in Zebra Chip Case." *Agricultural Research Magazine* 57, no. 9 (October 2009). http://www.ars.usda.gov/is/AR/archive/oct09/zebra1009.pdf.

———. "Multi-Pronged Fight against Zebra Chip Disease in Potatoes." *Agricultural Research Magazine* 60, no. 2 (February 2012). http://www.ars.usda.gov/is/AR/archive/feb12/potatoes0212.pdf.

U.S. International Trade Commission (USITC). Interactive Tariff and Trade DataWeb (DataWeb). http://dataweb.usitc.gov (accessed March 18, 2013).

———. *Small and Medium-Sized Enterprises: Characteristics and Performance*. USITC Publication 4189. Washington, DC: USITC, November 2010.

———. *Small and Medium-Sized Enterprises: Overview of Participation in U.S. Exports*. USITC Publication 4125. Washington, DC: USITC, January 2010.

———. *Small and Medium-Sized Enterprises: U.S. and EU Export Activities, and Barriers and Opportunities Experienced by U.S. Firms.* USITC Publication 4169. Washington, DC: USITC, July 2010.

———. *U.S.-Korea Free Trade Agreement: Potential Economy-wide and Selected Sectoral Effects.* USITC Publication 3949. Washington, DC: USITC, September 2007.

U.S. Trade Representative (USTR). "Korea." *2013 National Trade Estimate Report on Foreign Trade Barriers*. Washington, DC: USTR, 2013.

———. "New Opportunities for U.S. Exporters under the U.S.-Korea Trade Agreement." http://www.ustr.gov/trade-agreements/free-trade-agreements/korus-fta (accessed April 16, 2013).

World Integrated Trade Solution (WITS). UN Comtrade database (accessed March 18, 2013).

APPENDIX A. REQUEST LETTER

DOCKET NUMBER
2937
Office of the Secretary
Int'l Trade Commission

EXECUTIVE OFFICE OF THE PRESIDENT
THE UNITED STATES TRADE REPRESENTATIVE
WASHINGTON, D.C. 20508

RECEIVED
OFC OF THE SECRETARY
US INT'L TRADE COMM
2013 JAN 30 AM 10: 35

JAN 29 2013

The Honorable Irving A. Williamson
Chairman
U.S. International Trade Commission
500 E Street, S.W.
Washington, DC 20436

Dear Chairman Williamson:

One of the primary goals of the President's National Export Initiative is to increase export opportunities for America's small and medium-sized enterprises (SMEs), and expand exports from SMEs. In line with this initiative, the United States and Korea established a Working Group on SMEs under the United States-Korea Free Trade Agreement (KORUS). As indicated in the October 30, 2011 exchange of letters establishing the Working Group, two of its most important tasks are to (1) analyze and evaluate the impact of the implementation of the KORUS on production, distribution, and trade by SMEs, and (2) explore and develop ways for SMEs to take greater advantage of the economic opportunities created by the KORUS. Within one year of the Working Group's first meeting on June 5, 2012, the Working Group will present the outcome of its work to the KORUS's minister-level Joint Committee.

The KORUS SME Working Group convened two meetings in 2012, and the Working Group views it as useful for both Parties to conduct additional research to ascertain what information is available on the impact of the KORUS thus far on SMEs. The Government of Korea has commissioned a study aimed at investigating the impact of KORUS on exports of Korean SMEs to the United States. I believe that for the Working Group to be able to present effective recommendations to the Joint Committee with respect to possible ways to help U.S. SMEs take advantage of the new opportunities KORUS has created, the United States should also conduct a similar investigation, recognizing the constraints posed by the data at hand due to the short time period in which the KORUS has been in effect.

Therefore, pursuant to authority delegated by the President to the United States Trade Representative (USTR) under section 332(g) of the Tariff Act of 1930 (19 U.S.C. 1332(g)), I request that the Commission conduct an investigation and prepare a report containing information that will assist the Working Group in better understanding the impact of the KORUS on U.S. SMEs since its entry into force on March 15, 2012.

I request that the Commission, to the extent practicable, provide a report discussing the effects of the KORUS on the production, distribution, and export strategy of U.S. SMEs, as identified by those SMEs, and describing how U.S. SMEs have benefited from specific provisions of the KORUS, as well as challenges that U.S. SMEs may have faced in exporting to Korea. Such provisions may include but are not limited to those related to trade in goods and services or to intellectual property issues. The report should be based on available information, including information furnished by SMEs and interested parties following the Commission's notice of investigation. The U.S. SME sectors examined may include some or all of the business sectors listed in the three prior Commission reports on SMEs released in 2010, or other appropriate business sectors for which information is available.

I request that the report be delivered by May 1, 2013. As we intend to make the Commission's report available to the public, the report should not include confidential business or national security classified information.

I appreciate the Commission's assistance and cooperation in this matter.

Sincerely,

Ambassador Ron Kirk

APPENDIX B. SUMMARY OF POSITIONS OF INTERESTED PARTIES

The U.S. International Trade Commission (USITC or Commission) invited interested persons to file written submissions for this investigation.

This appendix summarizes the views expressed to the Commission via written submissions and oral statements and reflects the principal points made by the particular party. The views expressed in the summarized materials should be considered to be those of the submitting parties and not of the Commission. In preparing this summary, Commission staff did not undertake to confirm the accuracy of the information summarized or otherwise correct it. For the full text of written submissions, see entries associated with investigation no. 332-539 at the Commission's Electronic Docket Information System (https://edis.usitc.gov/edis3- internal/app).

American Association of Independent Music (A2IM)[1]

In a written submission, A2IM President Richard Bengloff said that A2IM is an organization of more than 300 independent music labels from across the United States, all of which are small and medium-sized enterprises (SMEs). Mr. Bengloff stated that although most A2IM members are small in terms of revenue, their contribution to the diversity of American music is enormous: at the 2013 Grammy Awards, for example, independent labels and artists won Album of the Year as well as Best Album awards in 18 different categories, and received more than 50 percent of all non-producer nominations.

According to Mr. Bengloff, in September 2012, A2IM and 15 of its SME members participated in a trade mission that, for the first time, included Seoul. Mr. Bengloff stated that the goal of the trip was to expand business opportunities for SME independent labels. Mr. Bengloff noted that delegates from prominent independent labels such as Ultra Music, the world's largest electronic dance music label; ATO Records, whose artists include Alabama Shakes; 335 Records (Grammy award-winning artist Larry Carlton); and VP Records (Sean Paul) met with Korean artists and entrepreneurs. Mr. Bengloff noted that A2IM members' meetings included one-on-one discussions to identify collaboration opportunities in such areas as recorded music sales (physical and digital), subscription services, synchronization licensing, and touring and merchandising, and involved 25–30 prospective buyers across these targeted areas. He added that the mission was organized by the U.S. Commercial Service Korea and included a networking dinner reception hosted by U.S. Ambassador to Korea Sung Y. Kim.

Mr. Bengloff said that A2IM members found a vibrant Korean music scene, bolstered by strong Korean government efforts to combat online piracy as part of the implementation of the U.S.-Korea Free Trade Agreement (FTA).

He stated that Korean businesses were very interested in importing A2IM members' intellectual property. The biggest ongoing challenge, Mr. Bengloff said, was low prices for digital downloads, as little as 5 cents a song, although A2IM expects prices to increase. Since the visit, many A2IM members have entered into agreements with their Korean counterparts, according to Mr. Bengloff. He added that although these types of arrangements can have a long gestation period, A2IM expects to see positive results for its members from improved conditions in the Korean market.

Coalition for a Prosperous America (CPA)[2]

In a written submission, CPA stated that it is a national, nonprofit organization comprising agriculture, manufacturing, and labor association and company members. According to the submission, CPA members are domestic supply chain companies with customers in the U.S. aerospace, automotive, electronics, medical, energy, defense, telecommunications, and other industries. CPA members also include SMEs from the tooling, machining, plastic mold building, steel, copper, aluminum, electronic component, and other industries. According to CPA, most CPA members do not export, and those that export do so on a limited basis.

CPA stated that it believes that the questions posed for the subject investigation are "not carefully tailored to gain facts relating to economic benefits or harm" resulting from the FTA. The coalition raised the following objections to the study request:

- The questions posed in the investigation are directed only to SME producers that export. SMEs generally do not export, and the U.S. domestic market is the largest and wealthiest market that is "feasible" for SME sales.
- The investigation is based on the assumption that, as a result of U.S. FTAs, domestic SME supply chain suppliers will benefit by exporting in the same way that original equipment manufacturers (OEMs) benefit from such agreements. Also, it assumes that the OEMs' supply chains will enjoy increased opportunities under such FTAs to supply those OEMs. CPA believes that competing nations pursue trade strategies and agreements to enable them to capture the supply chains of key industries and not open their markets to U.S. suppliers.

CPA said that it believes that CPA members in the domestic supply chain have been harmed by the FTA. According to CPA, U.S. FTAs in general have caused members to lose business to firms in other countries and have encouraged the relocation of U.S. supply chains offshore. CPA also states that the FTA does not include provisions to neutralize currency manipulation, border-adjustable value-added taxes, and state-controlled company subsidies.

Motor & Equipment Manufacturers Association (MEMA)[3]

In a written submission, Ann Wilson, senior vice president for government affairs, stated that MEMA represents more than 1,000 companies that produce motor vehicle parts for use in the light- and heavy-duty vehicle original equipment and aftermarket industries. She stated that motor vehicle parts manufacturers directly employ more than 734,000 workers and that the industry generates another 1.27 million indirect supply chain jobs.

Ms. Wilson stated that MEMA supported the passage of the FTA and that suppliers who have been active in the Korean market since before the FTA's entry into force hope to gain greater benefits from the agreement. She reported that MEMA canvassed members of its Small and Medium Enterprise Presidents Council concerning the FTA and found that no significant issues had been caused by the agreement, although one member company reported that it had lost business to a competitor in Korea since the FTA came into force.

Ms. Wilson said that MEMA has been working with the U.S. government regarding its concerns over Korea's new Vehicle Parts Self-Certification System. She stated that the issue involves the ability of U.S. firms to provide motor vehicle replacement parts for U.S.-originating vehicles exported to Korea. Under the FTA, according to Ms. Wilson, vehicles that comply with U.S. federal motor vehicle safety standards (FMVSS) are deemed to be compliant with comparable Korean standards, and U.S. replacement parts for U.S. vehicles exported to Korea would seemingly be a "non-issue"; however, Korea initially required imported U.S. motor vehicle parts to be certified to Korean standards, which are different from U.S. standards and would likely require manufacturers to retool their operations at a high cost. Ms. Wilson said that parts compliant with U.S. FMVSS should be granted equivalency to corresponding Korean standards.

Ms. Wilson asserted that the requirement of a "KC" stamp on each motor vehicle part under proposed Korean regulations would have been very burdensome to parts suppliers. In lieu of the stamp, however, she reported that final regulations allow the use of a sticker either on the part or on its packaging, as long as the replacement part meets the same U.S. FMVSS specifications as the original component. Although she stated that MEMA believes the U.S. FMVSS "DOT" mark should be sufficient for the Korean market, the use of the "KC" sticker is preferable to the stamp requirement.

Ms. Wilson also noted that U.S. parts manufacturers will be allowed to supply safety-related aftermarket parts only through the vehicle manufacturers' distribution network— that of Ford, GM, and Chrysler—while independent U.S. aftermarket suppliers are shut out of the market. According to Ms. Wilson, Korea may be concerned about counterfeit, low-cost, or low-quality parts entering the supply chain from non-U.S. sources. She contended that the safety standards that U.S. parts are required to meet should satisfy Korean concerns and that Korea should accommodate legitimate, independent U.S. aftermarket suppliers. Moreover, she said that MEMA has advocated for the use of quality motor vehicle parts both in original equipment and aftermarket installations and has urged the entire aftermarket industry to provide consumers with quality parts from manufacturing through distribution and repair.

Northwest Horticulture Council (NHC)[4]

In a written submission, Mark Powers, NHC vice president, stated that the NHC represents growers, packers, and shippers of tree fruit in the Pacific Northwest on national and international policy issues. Mr. Powers said that cherries are the only Pacific Northwest tree fruit exported to Korea. Exports of U.S. cherries to Korea have expanded by 86 percent, in large part because of the FTA provision reducing the relevant Korean tariff from 24 percent to zero. According to Mr. Powers, however, despite the tariff elimination and the resulting rise in demand in the Korean market, Korean regulatory challenges restrict U.S. cherry exports to Korea. Mr. Powers stated that Korea's requirement that cherries be fumigated with methyl bromide lessens product quality and limits the fruit's shelf life. He expressed the NHC's hope that a systems approach protocol can be agreed on to resolve the issue and find an alternative treatment to methyl bromide fumigation. [5] Mr. Powers also stated that Korea's process for monitoring chemical residues causes delays in processing cherry shipments at the port, disrupting markets and lowering fruit quality even in circumstances where evidence of residue violations does not exist. Finally, he stated that the entry into force of the FTA has not benefited U.S. apple and pear exporters because these fruits lack meaningful market access, due to long-standing Korean phytosanitary concerns, and this lack has not changed or been addressed.

United States Wine Institute and Wine America[6]

In a written submission, James B. Clawson of JBC International stated that the United States Wine Institute is a public policy and advocacy group representing more than 1,000 Californian wineries and affiliated businesses, and that Wine America (National Association of American Wineries) represents more than 800 wineries in 48 states. Mr. Clawson stated that the FTA's elimination of the 15 percent tariff on U.S. wine has made it possible for U.S. wine exporters to compete with Chilean and European producers in the Korean market. He said that Chilean and European exporters received duty-free access to the Korean market before U.S. exporters because their respective trade agreements with Korea entered into force before the U.S.-Korea FTA did, reducing market share in Korea for U.S. wine. He stated that the tariff reduction has not provided a competitive advantage for U.S. wine in the Korean market, but it has given U.S. wine parity with imported wines from Chile and the European Union. He also noted that Korea maintains a complicated tax and regulatory structure for the distribution of wine, which is a challenge that small U.S. exporters lack the resources to overcome. He said that, despite these challenges, U.S. wine exports to Korea increased by 40 percent in value between 2011 and 2012 "because of the effects" of the FTA.[7]

End Notes for Section 1

[1] For a copy of the letter requesting this report, see Appendix A.

[2] Based on the terms of the agreement as negotiated in 2007. See USITC, *U.S.-Korea Free Trade Agreement: Potential Economy-wide and Selected Sectoral Effects*, September 2007, xix.

[3] USTR, "New Opportunities for U.S. Exporters" (accessed April 10, 2013).

[4] USITC, *Small and Medium-Sized Enterprises: Overview of Participation*, January 2010; USITC, *Small and Medium-Sized Enterprises: U.S. and EU Export Activities*, July 2010; USITC, *Small and Medium-Sized Enterprises: Characteristics and Performance*, November 2010.

[5] USITC, *Small and Medium-Sized Enterprises: Overview of Participation*, January 2010, 3-1.

[6] The January 2010 USITC report on SMEs observed that several U.S. government agencies, including the Small Business Administration, the U.S. Department of Agriculture, and

Census, define small businesses in various industries using a variety of employee, revenue, and asset criteria. These size categories, however, define which firms are "small businesses" relative to specific industries, rather than the economy as a whole. Because this report analyzes the role of SMEs throughout the economy, the Commission has employed an economy-wide, rather than industry-specific, definition of SMEs. USITC, *Small and Medium-Sized Enterprises: Overview of Participation*, January 2010, 1-2 to 1-5.

[7] For summaries of the public submissions for this report, see Appendix B. The Commission scheduled a public hearing to collect information, but the hearing was canceled when the only request from an interested party to appear at the hearing was withdrawn.

End Notes for Section 2

[1] International Monetary Fund (IMF), *World Economic Outlook*, October 2012.

[2] GTIS, Global Trade Atlas database (accessed March 18, 2013). All trade data represent trade in goods, as data for trade in services for the periods examined are not available.

[3] GTIS, Global Trade Atlas database (accessed March 18, 2013).

[4] IMF, *Balance of Payments Statistics: Yearbook 2012*, 2012, 1033.

[5] Ibarra-Caton and Sharma, "U.S. International Services," October 2012, 36–37.

[6] Bloomberg, "Korea Output Unexpectedly Falls," July 30, 2012.

[7] Korean exports to the EU dropped by 11.4 percent from 2011 to 2012, while exports to China experienced only a slight increase of 0.1 percent following an increase of 14.9 percent in 2011. GTIS, Global Trade Atlas database (accessed March 18, 2013).

End Notes for Section 3

[1] This term denotes potatoes that are specifically designated to be processed into potato chips and not eaten fresh ("table-stock potatoes"), although chip-stock potatoes are also exported in a fresh state without having been processed.

[2] Under its most-favored-nation (MFN) obligations, imports into Korea of non-seed fresh potatoes, including chip-stock and table-stock potatoes, are subject to a TRQ, under which the first 18,810 mt of potatoes (in-quota imports) enter Korea at a rate of duty of 30 percent ad valorem, and imports over that amount (over-quota imports) enter at a rate of duty of 304 percent ad valorem. Under the FTA, Korea agreed (1) to provide separately for originating U.S. imports of chip-stock potatoes and table-stock potatoes and (2) to reduce its duties on some U.S. imports. For eligible imports of U.S. chip-stock potatoes, Korea agreed to immediately allow such imports to enter free of duty between December 1 and April 30 of each year. For imports of U.S. chip-stock potatoes entered between May 1 and November 30, Korea may initially impose its MFN rate of duty of 304 percent ad valorem, but Korea has agreed to reduce the duty in stages starting in 2019, with duty-free entry starting in 2026. For eligible U.S. imports of table-stock potatoes, Korea agreed to allow the first 3,000 mt of U.S. imports of such potatoes to enter duty free during the first year of the FTA, with all imports above that quantity subject to the MFN rate of duty of 304 percent ad valorem. Korea agreed to increase the 3,000 mt trigger quantity for the TRQ at the rate of 3 percent per year.

[3] Company representative, telephone interview by USITC staff, March 19, 2013.

[4] Zebra chip disease is a bacteriological infection that affects product quality but is not harmful to humans. Suszkiw, "Bacterium Identified as Prime Suspect," October 2009, 22; Suszkiw, "Multi-Pronged Fight against Zebra Chip Disease in Potatoes," February 2012, 8–9.

[5] Strebin Farms stated that U.S. table-stock potato exporters should be able to ship their product to Korea if it is first certified as being free from the disease and the potato psyllid—the vector that infects potato plants with the bacterium that causes zebra chip disease. Company representative, telephone interview by USITC staff, March 18, 2013.

[6] Company representative, telephone interview by USITC staff, March 20, 2013.

[7] Company representative, telephone interview by USITC staff, March 19, 2013.

[8] Ibid.

[9] Company representative, telephone interview by USITC staff, March 18, 2013.

[10] Company representative, telephone interview by USITC staff, March 20, 2013.

[11] Korean imports of hay and other fodder of subheading 1214.90 (except alfalfa in bales) has an MFN duty rate of 100.6 percent ad valorem. Imports within the TRQ trigger quantity of 200,000 mt set by the FTA can enter free of duty; that quantity applies for the first 14 years of the FTA and is then unlimited. Over-quota shipments are accorded 15-year staged duty reductions from the MFN rate. Alfalfa in bales is accorded 5- year staged duty reductions from the MFN rate of 18 percent ad valorem. Sweetened animal forage of subheading 2309.90 is also subject to a TRQ if considered supplemental animal feeds, with a 5,500 mt trigger quantity increasing incrementally each year to 7,392 mt in year 11 and unlimited as of year 12, with over-quota imports accorded 12-year staged duty reductions from the base rate. Goods of subheading 2309.90 are subject to MFN duty rates of 6.6 percent or 60.6 percent ad valorem, depending on the type and additives.

[12] Anderson Hay & Grain is a Washington state company with additional locations in Oregon and California. They specialize in the production and export of hay, including timothy hay, alfalfa hay, and grass straw products, to be used as feed for horses and cattle.

[13] Most U.S. exports to Korea of hay and fodder products were subject to a tariff of 100.5 percent before the entry into force of the FTA.

[14] Anderson Hay & Grain Co., written submission to the USITC, March 26, 2013; company representative, email message to USITC staff, April 3, 2013.

[15] Company representative, telephone interview by USITC staff, March 20, 2013.

[16] Apples and pears were accorded either 7- or 10-year staged duty reductions from the MFN duty rate of 46 percent ad valorem, depending on the variety being imported.

[17] Company representative, telephone interview by USITC staff, March 28, 2013.

[18] Company representative, telephone interview by USITC staff, March 27, 2013.

[19] Company representative, telephone interview by USITC staff, March 20, 2013.

[20] Systems approach protocols vary by product, but typically include a number of processes that mitigate pest risk and allow the importation of the specific product under an acceptable level of phytosanitary security.

[21] Company representative, telephone interview by USITC staff, March 28, 2013.

[22] Company representative, telephone interview by USITC staff, March 20, 2013; company representative, telephone interview by USITC staff, March 27, 2013. See USITC, *U.S.-Korea Free Trade Agreement: Potential Economy-wide and Selected Sectoral Effects*, September 2007, 3-21.

[23] Company representative, telephone interview by USITC staff, March 27, 2013.

[24] Ibid.

[25] Company representative, telephone interview by USITC staff, March 28, 2013.

[26] Company representative, telephone interview by USITC staff, March 20, 2013.

[27] Wente Vineyards of Livermore, California, is one of the oldest continually operating, family-owned wineries in the United States.

[28] A company representative stated that it is very difficult to compete on price with Chilean exporters, who are the low-cost suppliers in the Korean market because of their low production costs and duty-free access, but that the FTA's entry into force has reduced the retail price differential. In addition, the representative said that although wines from Europe still dominate the Korean market, the tariff reduction has made U.S. exports more cost competitive against European wines, which also benefit from duty-free access as a result of the EU-Korea FTA. Company representative, telephone interview by USITC staff, March 12, 2013.

[29] Ibid.

[30] Silver Oak produces Cabernet wines from grapes grown on its own vineyards as well as from grapes grown by a small group of independent growers.

[31] Company representative, telephone interview by USITC staff, March 20, 2013.

[32] Company representative, telephone interview by USITC staff, March 12, 2013.

[33] Ibid.

[34] Company representative, telephone interview by USITC staff, March 20, 2013.

[35] Optimum Spring Solutions specializes in springs made of high-temperature and specialty alloys including stainless steel, nickel, copper, and cobalt alloys.

[36] Company representative, telephone interview by USITC staff, March 18, 2013.

[37] Under the FTA, the MFN duty rates ranging up to 8.6 percent ad valorem were eliminated immediately on originating goods.

[38] AAMSI provides structural component and assembly manufacturing, parts repair, and overhaul, among other services.

[39] Company representative, telephone interview by USITC staff, March 14, 2013.

[40] Company representative, telephone interview by USITC staff, March 18, 2013.

[41] Company representatives, telephone interview by USITC staff, April 5, 2013.

[42] Company representative, telephone interview by USITC staff, March 18, 2013.

[43] Korea has made progress in IP protection and enforcement during the negotiation and implementation of the FTA. Three reforms are particularly relevant to the protection of music. In 2009, the Korean government amended the copyright law to deter copyright infringement over Internet file-sharing platforms. In 2010, it provided for sanctions against repeat infringers under its "three strikes" law. In 2011, it passed a law requiring online storage lockers to register with the Korea Communications Commission, facilitating online IP enforcement. The Korean government also has dedicated increased resources to improving enforcement on the ground. USTR, "Korea," 2013, 237.

[44] The trade mission was arranged by the American Association of Independent Music (A2IM), an industry association of independent music labels. See Appendix B for a summary of its comments in this investigation.

[45] CMJ Holdings Corp., written submission to the USITC, April 9, 2013.

[46] A company representative noted that the Korean market was open to "traditional business practices," in which artists enter into agreements and get paid pursuant to those agreements. Company representative, telephone interview by USITC staff, March 11, 2013.

[47] DiSTI exports to roughly 40 countries and has been growing its business in Korea for the last seven years, using a Korean partner company to act as its agent to assist with language and cultural barriers.

[48] Company representative, email message to USITC staff, March 28, 2013.

[49] Ibid.

End Notes for Appendix B

[1] A2IM, written submission to the USITC, April 8, 2013.

[2] CPA, written submission to the USITC, March 25, 2013; CPA executive and members, meeting with USITC staff, Washington, DC, March 14, 2013.

[3] MEMA, written submission to the USITC, March 25, 2013.

[4] NHC, written submission to the USITC, March 22, 2013.

[5] Systems approach protocols vary by product, but typically include a number of processes that mitigate pest risk and allow the importation of the specific product under an acceptable level of phytosanitary security.

[6] JBC International on behalf of the United States Wine Institute and Wine America, written submission to the USITC, March 25, 2013.

[7] JBC International on behalf of the United States Wine Institute and Wine America, written submission to the USITC, March 25, 2013, 4.

In: Effects of U.S.-Korea Free Trade Agreement … ISBN: 978-1-62808-843-4
Editor: Brian M. Sullivan

Chapter 2

THE U.S.-SOUTH KOREA FREE TRADE AGREEMENT (KORUS FTA): PROVISIONS AND IMPLICATIONS*

William H. Cooper, Mark E. Manyin, Remy Jurenas and Michaela D. Platzer

SUMMARY

On October 3, 2011, President Obama submitted draft legislation (H.R. 3080/S. 1642) to implement the U.S.-South Korea Free Trade Agreement (KORUS FTA) to both houses of Congress. On October 6, the House Ways and Means Committee reported out H.R. 3080 (H.Rept. 112-239). The Senate Finance Committee reported out S. 1642 (without written report). On October 12, the House passed H.R. 3080 (278-151) and sent it to the Senate which passed it (83- 15). The President signed the legislation on October 21, 2011 (P.L. 112-41). In South Korea, after a contentious battle, the Korean National Assembly passed the agreement on November 22. On March 15, 2012, the KORUS FTA entered into force.

The KORUS FTA is the second-largest U.S. FTA (next to NAFTA). South Korea is the seventh-largest trading partner of the United States, and the United States is South Korea's third-largest trading partner. The KORUS FTA covers a wide range of trade and investment issues and,

---

* This is an edited, reformatted and augmented version of Congressional Research Service, Publication No. RL34330, dated March 7, 2013.

therefore, could have substantial economic implications for both the United States and South Korea.

Congress approved the KORUS FTA implementing legislation using expedited procedures authorized by the Trade Promotion Authority (TPA). Under TPA, the President had the discretion on when to submit the implementing legislation to Congress. The KORUS FTA was negotiated and signed on June 30, 2007, by President George W. Bush. However, President Bush did not submit the legislation because of differences with the Democratic leadership over treatment of autos and beef, among other issues. On December 3, 2010, after a series of arduous negotiations, President Obama and President Lee announced that they had reached an agreement on addressing the outstanding issues related to the KORUS FTA. As a result, U.S. and South Korean negotiators agreed, in the form of an exchange of letters and agreed minutes, to modifications to the commitments made in the 2007 agreement. These modifications included changes in phase-out periods for tariffs on autos and pork, a new safeguard provision on autos, and concessions by South Korea on allowing a larger number of U.S. cars into South Korea under U.S. safety standards than was the case under the original KORUS FTA provisions. The modifications were included in the implementing legislation.

A broad swath of the U.S. business community supported the KORUS FTA. With the modifications in the commitments reached in December 2010, this group also included the three Detroit-based auto manufacturers and the United Auto Workers (UAW) union. It still faced opposition from some labor unions and other groups, including Public Citizen. Many U.S. supporters view the KORUS FTA as important to secure new opportunities in the South Korean market, while opponents claimed that the KORUS FTA does not go far enough to break down South Korean trade barriers or that the agreement will encourage U.S. companies to move their production offshore at the expense of U.S. workers. Other observers suggested the KORUS FTA could have implications for the U.S.-South Korean alliance as a whole, as well as on U.S. Asia policy and U.S. trade policy.

INTRODUCTION

On October 3, 2011, President Obama submitted draft legislation (H.R. 3080/S. 1642) to implement the U.S.-South Korea Free Trade Agreement (KORUS FTA) to both houses of Congress. On October 6, the House Ways and Means Committee reported out H.R. 3080 (H.Rept. 112-239). The Senate Finance Committee reported out S. 1642 (without written report). On October 12, the House passed H.R. 3080 (278-151) and sent it to the Senate which passed it (83-15). The President signed the legislation on October 21, 2011 (P.L. 112-41). In South Korea, after a contentious battle, the Korean National Assembly passed the agreement on November 22. The KORUS FTA entered into force on March 15, 2012.

The KORUS FTA covers a wide range of bilateral economic activities: trade in manufactured goods, agricultural products, and services; foreign investment; government procurement; intellectual property rights; and worker rights and environment protection, among other issues.

The negotiations were conducted under the trade promotion authority (TPA), also called fast-track trade authority, that Congress granted the President under the Bipartisan Trade Promotion Act of 2002 (P.L. 107-210). Under TPA the President had the discretion on when to submit the implementing legislation to Congress. President Bush did not submit the legislation because of differences with the Democratic leadership over treatment of autos and beef, among other issues.

On December 3, 2010, U.S. and South Korean leaders announced that they had reached agreement on addressing the outstanding issues related to the KORUS FTA. As a result, U.S.-and South Korean negotiators agreed to modifications to some of the commitments made in the 2007 agreement. These modifications which were signed on February 10, 2011, are in the form of an "exchange of letters" and two "agreed minutes." They pertain mostly to the auto provisions and include changes in phase-out periods for tariffs on autos and pork, a new safeguard provision on autos, and concessions by South Korea on allowing a larger number of U.S. cars into South Korea under U.S. safety standards than was the case under the original KORUS FTA provisions.

The United States and South Korea entered into the KORUS FTA as a means to further solidify an already strong economic relationship by reducing barriers to trade and investment between them and to resolve long-standing troublesome economic issues. The United States specifically sought increased access to South Korean markets for agricultural products, services, and foreign investment. For South Korean leaders, the KORUS FTA is a mechanism to promote reform in its own economy and also to gain a competitive advantage in the U.S. market for autos and other manufactured goods.

Supporters of the FTA in the United States argued that failure to approve the KORUS FTA would have allowed those opportunities to slip away, particularly if Seoul's strategy of negotiating a web of FTAs, with South Korea at the center, is successful. On July 1, 2011, South Korea's FTA with the European Union (EU) went into effect. However, some opponents of the KORUS FTA argued that the agreement as originally concluded in June 2007 failed to go far enough in addressing South Korean trade barriers and would have been a lost opportunity if approved in its current form.

Presidents Obama's Statements on the KORUS FTA

President Obama and South Korean President Lee Myung-bak met for the first time on April 2, 2009, in London on the sidelines of the G-20 summit. Afterward, an Obama Administration official said that President Obama told Lee he wants to "make progress" on the agreement, and that the two leaders agreed that the two countries' staffs should "discuss how to move forward."[1]

The two presidents met again on June 16, 2009, in Washington, DC. In a joint statement released at the summit, they said: "We will continue to deepen our strong bilateral economic, trade and investment relations. We recognize that the Korea-U.S. (KORUS) Free Trade Agreement could further strengthen these ties and we are committed to working together to chart a way forward." In answering a question at a joint press conference, President Obama stated, "What I have done is to affirm to [South Korean] President Lee that we want to work constructively with the Republic of Korea in a systematic way to clear some of these barriers that are preventing free trade from occurring between our two countries."[2] However, President Obama did not indicate a timeframe for consideration of legislation to implement the KORUS FTA.

At a joint press conference with President Lee in Seoul in November 2009, President Obama said the agreement "holds out the promise of serving our mutual interests. And together, we're committed to working together to move the agreement forward." President Lee said the two leaders agreed to "redouble" their efforts toward this end.[3] Prior to his meeting with President Lee, President Obama said in a Fox News interview that "I want to get the deal done.... Overall, I think it's a potential good deal for US exporters. But there's certain sectors of the economy that aren't dealt with as effectively and that's something that I'm going to be talking to President Lee about."[4]

During his January 27, 2010, State of the Union address, President Obama, without mentioning the KORUS FTA per se, expressed the need for the United States to strengthen its trade ties in Asia "with partners like South Korea." During a question-and-answer session at the January 29, 2010, House Republican issues conference, the President referred to the need to seize trade opportunities, mentioning South Korea in particular.

On June 26, 2010, President Obama announced that he would direct U.S. Trade Representative Ron Kirk to work with the South Korean trade minister to resolve outstanding issues on the KORUS FTA by the time President Obama and South Korean President Lee meet again in Seoul in November 2010 for the G-20 summit. The President said that he intends "in the few months" after the November meeting to present Congress with the implementing legislation for the agreement. The President made the announcement at a joint press conference following his meeting with President Lee prior to the G-20 summit in Toronto.

On November 11, 2010, in Seoul, after the two presidents announced that the two sides had not resolved the outstanding issues, President Obama said that the U.S. and South Korean negotiating teams would be working "in the coming days and weeks ahead" to reach agreement. He said that an FTA "done right" would be a "win-win" for both countries.

On December 4, 2010, President Obama announced that U.S. and South Korean negotiators had reached agreement on modifications to the KORUS FTA making the agreement a win for the United States and for "our ally and friend" South Korea.

On July 8, 2011, the President made the following remarks as part of his statement on the latest U.S. employment report: "There are bills and trade agreements before Congress right now that could get all these ideas moving. All of them have bipartisan support. All of them could pass immediately. And I urge Congress not to wait. The American people need us to do everything we can to help strengthen this economy and make sure that we are producing more jobs."

On October 13, 2011, at a joint news conference with President Lee Myung-bak on the occasion of the latter's state visit to Washington, President Obama said: "... just as Americans buy Hyundais and Kias, I hope that South Koreans will buy more Fords, Chryslers and Chevys.... The KORUS FTA] will boost American exports by up to $11 billion and support some 70,000 American jobs. It has groundbreaking protections for labor rights, the environment and intellectual property—so that trade is free and fair. It will promote green jobs and clean energy, another area where we're deepening our cooperation. And it keeps us on track to achieve my goals of doubling American exports."

A congressionally mandated study by the United States International Trade Commission (USITC) concluded that investment and trade between the United States and South Korea would increase modestly as a result of the

KORUS FTA.[5] This result was in line with other similar studies. In general and in the short-to-medium term, the KORUS FTA's largest commercial effects are expected to be microeconomic in nature. The U.S. services and agriculture industries, for instance, are expected to reap significant benefits from the agreement.

Many observers have argued that in addition to its economic implications, the KORUS FTA will have diplomatic and security implications. For example, they have suggested that it will deepen the U.S.-South Korean alliance. The United States and South Korea have been allies since the United States intervened on the Korean Peninsula in 1950 and fought to repel a North Korean takeover of South Korea. Over 33,000 U.S. troops were killed and over 100,000 were wounded during the three-year conflict.[6] South Korea subsequently has assisted U.S. deployments in other conflicts, most recently by deploying over 3,000 troops to play a non-combat role in Iraq. However, some counter this by positing that the KORUS FTA need not be seen as a necessary, let alone sufficient, condition for enhancing the U.S.-ROK alliance. Mutual interests on critical issues pertaining to North Korea and the rest of the region will continue to require close cooperation between the two countries in the national security sphere.

This report examines the provisions of the KORUS FTA in the context of the overall U.S.-South Korean economic relationship, U.S. objectives, and South Korean objectives. It also examines some of the issues that have arisen during its implementation.

THE KORUS FTA IN A NUTSHELL

Some highlights of the results of the agreement are provided below. Background information and a more detailed examination of the agreement's provisions are provided in the main sections of this report.

Agriculture

Under the KORUS FTA's agricultural provisions, South Korea immediately granted duty-free status to almost two-thirds of current U.S. agricultural exports. Tariffs and import quotas on most other agricultural goods will be phased out within 10 years, with a few commodities and food products subject to provisions that phase out such protection by year 23.

However, because of their sensitivity, access for several U.S. products will slowly expand in perpetuity but remain subject to South Korean import quotas.

Much effort went into negotiating provisions covering three agricultural commodities of export interest to the United States. Under the KORUS FTA, South Korea agreed to eliminate its 40% tariff on beef muscle meats imported from the United States over a 15-year period. However, negotiators did not reach a breakthrough by the end of the talks on the separate but parallel issue of how to resolve differences on the terms of access for all U.S. beef in a way that would address Korea's human health concerns arising from the 2003 discovery of mad cow disease in the U.S. cattle herd. Though sales of U.S. boneless beef from cattle aged less than 30 months did resume in April 2007 under a separate agreement reached in early 2006, sales of bone-in beef (e.g., ribs) only began in July 2008 after the conclusion of a difficult series of negotiations—accompanied by widespread public protests in Korea—on a more comprehensive agreement. Under the terms of a commercial understanding sanctioned by both governments, exports are limited to all cuts of beef (boneless and bone-in) from cattle less than 30 months old when slaughtered. Both countries view this "voluntary private-sector" arrangement as a transitional step intended to improve Korean consumer confidence in U.S. beef.

Negotiations on access for U.S. rice and oranges into the South Korean market also were contentious. Rice was a "make-or-break" issue for Seoul, and excluded at South Korea's insistence out of U.S. recognition that if pushed, the talks would likely have collapsed. Special treatment for U.S. oranges was struck at the last moment, when negotiators compromised on a multi-part solution expected to increase U.S. navel orange exports over time. In the December 2010 changes to the initial agreement, Korea secured an extension in the tariff phase-out for one commercially important line of U.S. frozen pork product in return for changes the United States sought in its commitments under the auto and other provisions. In June 2011, South Korea's trade minister clarified that the use of generic names by U.S. cheese exporters selling to that market will not be restricted by provisions in the EU-Korea (KOREU) FTA.

Automobiles

Trade in autos and auto parts proved to be among the most difficult issues tackled by U.S. and South Korean negotiators. In recent years, South Korean auto manufacturers have increased their market share through imports and expanded car production in the United States and other major automotive markets like the European Union. U.S. industry argued that South Korea should eliminate policies and practices that seemingly discriminate against U.S. auto imports. In December 2010, the United States and South Korea reached a joint understanding on automotive trade.[7] Due to these modifications, all three U.S. automakers ultimately supported the KORUS FTA. A detailed discussion of the auto-specific provisions is provided later in this report. A few of the most important provisions are discussed below.

- The United States will eliminate its tariff of 2.5% on passenger cars, including electric and hybrid vehicles, as of 2016. South Korea cut its passenger car tariff to 4% upon implementation of the KORUS FTA and will remove the remaining tariff in 2016.[8] For trucks, South Korea dropped its 10% duty upon implementation, while the U.S. tariff of 25% will remain in place for seven years and then be phased out entirely by 2021. The KORUS FTA also includes a "snapback provision" that allows the United States to reinstate its 2.5% passenger car tariff, once the duties are completely eliminated, if U.S. automakers claim and the dispute settlement panel finds that South Korea is in violation of the agreement. The snapback could also be imposed due to violations regarding imports of trucks. South Korean commitments regarding a specified group of new and already proposed regulations on automobile fuel economy and greenhouse gas emissions do not seem to be enforceable under the dispute settlement provisions of the KORUS FTA; presumably the snapback will not apply to these commitments.[9]
- A special motor vehicle safeguard allows the United States to take action if there are "any harmful surges in South Korean auto imports due to the agreement." As a remedy under the auto-specific safeguard, the United States will be able to reimpose the 2.5% passenger vehicle tariff. However, a surge in automobile imports from South Korea seems unlikely as South Korean auto manufacturers have substantially increased their assembly production in the United States to about 720,000 cars and light trucks in 2012.[10] If U.S.-based producers–including foreign-owned automakers such as BMW or Toyota–meet U.S. federal safety standards, each manufacturer can export as many as 25,000 cars directly to South Korea from the United States without complying with South Korean safety standards. Additionally, they

must satisfy KORUS FTA domestic content provisions. U.S. automakers also have some flexibility to be considered in compliance with new South Korean fuel economy and greenhouse gas emissions standards.

Other Key Provisions

The KORUS FTA covers a broad range of other areas. According to the Office of the United States Trade Representative (USTR), 95% of U.S.-South Korean trade in *consumer and industrial products* will become duty-free by 2016 and virtually all remaining tariffs will be lifted by 2021. The two countries agreed to liberalize trade in *services* by opening up their markets beyond what they have committed to do in the World Trade Organization (WTO). About 60% of U.S.-South Korea trade in *textiles and apparel* became duty-free immediately, and the KORUS FTA will provide a special safeguard mechanism to reduce the impact of textile and apparel import surges.

Trade remedies were a critical issue for South Korea and a sensitive issue for the United States. The FTA allows for the United States to exempt imports from South Korea from a "global" escape clause (§201) measure if they are not a major cause of serious injury or a threat of serious injury to the U.S. domestic industry. The FTA also provided for a binational consultative committee for information sharing on trade remedy matters.[11]

In addition, South Korea and the United States agreed to establish an independent body, a Medicines and Medical Devices Committee, to review recommendations and determinations regarding South Korean pricing and government reimbursement for *pharmaceuticals and medical devices* and to improve transparency in the process for making those determinations.

Furthermore, one year after the KORUS FTA enters into force, a binational committee was to be formed to study the possibility of eventually expanding the agreement's coverage to products from "Outward Processing Zones," including the Kaesong Industrial Complex and/or other future zones located in North Korea. (That committee has not yet been formed.)

ESTIMATES OF THE OVERALL ECONOMIC EFFECTS OF A KORUS FTA

Economists have released several studies estimating the potential effects of the KORUS FTA. As required by the TPA statute, the USITC conducted a study in 2007 of the KORUS FTA at the request of the President.[12] The USITC study concluded that U.S. GDP will be higher by $10.1 billion to $11.9 billion (approximately 0.1%) when the KORUS FTA is fully implemented, a negligible amount given the size of the U.S. economy. The USITC based this estimate primarily on the removal of tariffs and tariff-rate-quotas, that is, barriers that can be relatively easily quantified. The study concluded that U.S. exports of goods will likely be higher by $9.7 billion to $10.9 billion, primarily in agricultural products, machinery, electronics, transportation equipment, including passenger vehicles and parts. U.S. imports will increase $6.4 billion to $6.9 billion, primarily in textiles, apparel, leather products, footwear, machinery, electronics, and passenger vehicles and parts.[13]

The range did not take into account the impact of the reduction of barriers to trade in services and to foreign investment flows and the impact of changes in regulations as a result of the KORUS FTA. The study noted that U.S. exports in services will increase as a result of South Korean commitments under the KORUS FTA, and that changes in the regulatory environment in both countries will also help to increase bilateral trade and investment flows.

The study estimated that changes in aggregate U.S. employment will be negligible given the much larger size of the U.S. economy compared to the South Korean economy. However, while some sectors, such as livestock producers, will experience increases in employment, others such as textile, wearing apparel, and electronic equipment manufacturers are expected to experience declines in employment.[14]

Other studies draw the same basic conclusions, although the magnitudes differ because they employ different models from the USITC study. For example, a University of Michigan analysis commissioned by the Korea Economic Institute estimated that U.S. GDP will increase by $25.12 billion (0.14% of U.S. GDP). This is larger than the USITC estimate, but in part this is because its authors quantified the effects of liberalization in services trade.[15] The authors also analyzed the impact of a KORUS FTA before the final text had been released and assumed, among other things, that rice trade would be liberalized, which, in the end, was not the case. In December 2005, the Korea Institute for International Economic Policy (KIEP) published a study measuring the potential economic impact of a U.S.-South Korean FTA on South Korea alone. The study estimated some of the dynamic, or long-run, economic effects in addition to the static, or one-time, effects of the FTA on South Korea. The KIEP study estimated that the FTA will eventually lead to a 0.42% to 0.59% increase in South Korea's GDP according to a static analysis, and 1.99% to 2.27% according to a dynamic analysis.[16]

AN OVERVIEW OF THE U.S.-SOUTH KOREAN ECONOMIC RELATIONSHIP

South Korea is a major economic partner for the United States. In 2012, two-way trade between the two countries totaled $101.1 billion, making South Korea the United States' seventh-largest trading partner. (See Table 1.) Major U.S. exports to South Korea include semiconductors, machinery (particularly semiconductor production machinery), aircraft, and agricultural products.

Table 1. Annual U.S.-South Korea Merchandise Trade, Selected Years (billions of U.S. dollars)

Year	U.S. Exports	U.S. Imports	Trade balance	Total trade
1990	14.4	18.5	-4.1	32.9
1995	25.4	24.2	1.2	49.6
2000	26.3	39.8	-13.5	66.1
2003	22.5	36.9	-14.4	59.5
2004	25.0	45.1	-20.1	70.1
2005	26.2	43.2	-17.0	69.4
2006	30.8	44.7	-13.9	75.5
2007	33.0	45.4	-12.4	78.4
2008	33.1	46.7	-13.6	79.8
2009	27.0	38.7	-11.7	65.7
2010	38.0	48.9	-10.9	86.9
2011	43.5	56.6	-13.1	100.
2012	42.3	58.9	-16.6	101.
Major U.S. Export Items	Industrial machinery; chemicals; semiconductor circuits; corn & wheat; specialized instruments.			
Major U.S. Import Items	Cell phones; semiconductor circuits; cars & car parts; iron & steel.			

Sources: 1990 and 1995 data from Global Trade Information Services. 2000-2008 data from U.S. International Trade Commission. The 2000-2012 U.S. export data are for U.S. domestic exports and the data for U.S. imports are for imports on a consumption basis.

South Korea is far more dependent economically on the United States than the United States is on South Korea. In 2012, the United States was South Korea's third-largest trading partner, second-largest export market, and the third-largest source of imports. In 2003, China for the first time displaced the United States from its perennial place as South Korea's number one trading partner. In 2005 Japan overtook the United States to become South Korea's second-largest trade partner.

Table 2. Asymmetrical Economic Interdependence (2012)

	Total Trade	Export Market	Source of Imports
For the U.S., South Korea ranks	# 7	# 8	# 6
For South Korea, U.S. ranks	# 3	# 2	# 3

Sources: U.S. Department of Commerce, U.S. Census Bureau and Bureau of Economic Analysis; Bank of Korea.

Increased economic interaction between the United States and South Korea has been accompanied by numerous disagreements over trade policies. In general, U.S. exporters and trade negotiators identify the lack of transparency of South Korea's trading and regulatory systems as the most significant barriers to trade with South Korea in almost every major product sector. Many U.S. government officials also complain that Seoul continues to use government regulations and standard-setting powers to discriminate against foreign firms in politically sensitive industries, such as automobiles and telecommunications. Another major cross-sectoral complaint is that rigidities in the South Korean labor market, such as mandatory severance pay, raise the cost of investing and doing business. Finally, the United States and other countries have pressed South Korea to open further its agricultural market, which is considered one of the most closed among members of the Organization for Economic Co-operation and Development (OECD).[17] Many of these issues arose during the KORUS FTA negotiations.

The intensity of these disputes has diminished considerably since the late 1980s and early 1990s, in part because South Korea enacted a set of sweeping market-oriented reforms as a *quid pro quo* for receiving a U.S.-led $58 billion package from the International Monetary Fund (IMF) following the near collapse of the South Korean economy in 1997. In particular, as a result of the reforms, South Korea opened its doors to foreign investors, ushering in billions of dollars of foreign portfolio and foreign direct investment (FDI). The result is that foreign companies, including U.S. firms, now are significant shareholders in many prominent industrial conglomerates (*chaebol*); at one point earlier in the decade, foreign firms owned about one-third of the South Korean banking industry and an estimated 40% of the value of the shares traded on South Korea's stock exchange. Since the 1997 crisis, FDI commitments by U.S. companies have totaled over $25 billion.[18]

Additionally, the United States and South Korea appear to have become more adept at managing their trade disputes. This may be partly due to the quarterly, working-level "trade action agenda" trade meetings that were initiated in early 2001. Both sides credit the meetings, which appear to be unique to the U.S.-South Korean trade relationship, with creating a more constructive dialogue that helped pave the way for the two sides to feel sufficiently confident to launch FTA negotiations.

U.S. AND SOUTH KOREAN OBJECTIVES IN AN FTA

U.S. and South Korean policymakers shared certain goals in launching and completing the negotiations on the KORUS FTA. Both governments saw in the FTA a logical extension of an already important economic relationship that would provide a means by which the two trading partners could address and resolve fundamental issues and, thereby, raise the relationship to a higher level. For the United States these issues have included the high tariffs and other restrictions on agricultural imports. For South Korea, these difficult issues have included perceived U.S. discrimination toward South Korean imports in the application of trade remedies and treatment of products made at the Kaesong Industrial Complex in North Korea.

While sharing some broad objectives, U.S. and South Korean leaders also approached the KORUS FTA from different perspectives that were reflected in the conduct and outcome of the negotiations. A primary objective of the United States was to gain access to South Korean markets in agricultural products, pharmaceuticals and medical equipment, some other high-technology manufactured goods, and services, particularly financial and professional services— areas in which U.S. producers are internationally competitive but for which South Korean barriers seemed to be high.

For South Korea, gaining a large increase in market access was not as critical a priority since South Korean exporters already have a significant presence in areas in which they have proved to be competitive—consumer electronics and autos, for example, and in which they already face only low or zero U.S. tariffs. However, South Korea sought to preserve its share of the U.S. market in the face of growing competition from emerging East Asian producers from Thailand, Malaysia, Vietnam, and possibly China. South Korea also aimed to improve its competitive position in the U.S. market vis-à-vis Japan where the elimination of even low tariffs might give South Korean exporters some price advantage.

Launching the FTA negotiations was largely at the initiative of South Korea. Its main objective in securing an FTA with the United States was much broader than gaining reciprocal access to the U.S. market. Entering an FTA with the United States meshed with a number of former South Korean President Roh Moo-hyun's long-term economic and strategic goals. Roh made an FTA the top economic priority for the remainder of his tenure, which ended in February 2008.[19] Soon after his election in 2002, Roh committed himself to raising South Korea's per capita gross domestic product (GDP) to $20,000 by the end of the decade and to transforming South Korea into a major "economic hub" in Northeast Asia by expanding the economic reforms begun by his predecessor following the 1997 Asian financial crisis. Ongoing competitive pressure from Japanese firms, increased competition from Chinese enterprises, and the rapid ageing of the South Korean workforce has heightened the sense of urgency about boosting national competitiveness. Continuing along this line of argument, ex-Prime Minister Han Duk-soo has said that a failure to adopt significant economic changes will mean that "Korea's long term growth potential is likely to deteriorate."[20] Former President Lee Myung-bak, who succeeded Roh in December 2007, made the economy the centerpiece of his campaign and supported the KORUS FTA as part of a larger program to promote South Korean economic growth.

During the negotiations, South Korean officials and other South Korean proponents of the KORUS FTA tended not to focus on the increased access to the U.S. market. Rather, they emphasized the medium and long-term gains that would stem from increased allocative efficiency of the South Korean economy, particularly in the services industries. This would presumably be brought about by an influx of U.S. investment and technology into South Korea and by the spur of increased competition with U.S. firms.[21] Senior officials in particular emphasized the need to boost the competitiveness of South Korean service industries. An FTA with the United States, they argued, will help address South Korea's increased economic polarization by spurring job creation in fields such as medical, legal, education, and accounting services.[22] Some, however, say an FTA will worsen South Korea's income gap.[23] Also, during the talks, there were continuous and often large scale anti-FTA protests, generally led by South Korean farmers and trade unionists.

The absence of mirror-image or reciprocal U.S. and South Korean objectives in the negotiations is reflected in the structure of the KORUS FTA. Except for some provisions dealing with issues specific to U.S.-South Korea economic relations, for example, South Korea taxation of autos and the Kaesong industrial complex, the structure of the KORUS FTA largely resembles the structure of other U.S. FTAs, such as Dominican Republic-Central American FTA (DR-CAFTA).This conclusion does not suggest that South Korea did not bring to the table its own specific demands, which it did (such as the exclusion of rice) and held to them firmly.

SECTOR-SPECIFIC ISSUES AND THE KORUS FTA

Under the KORUS FTA, the United States and South Korea agreed to eliminate tariffs on most manufactured goods immediately upon implementation and the others no later than year-end 2021. [24] The agreement also included provisions on sensitive sectors such as agricultural products and auto trade.

Agriculture and Sanitary and Phytosanitary Issues

Overview

Attaining comprehensive market access for U.S. agricultural products to South Korea's large market and finding a way to resolve South Korea's continued restrictions on U.S. beef purchases (imposed to protect human health following the late 2003 discovery of mad cow disease in the U.S. cattle herd) were the two primary objectives pursued by U.S. agricultural negotiators. Though South Korea ranks among the leading agricultural importing countries in the world, its farm sector is highly protected with high tariffs and quotas.[25] This reflects its farmers' longstanding political influence (particularly that of rice producers) and its urban population's deep ties to its rural roots.

In concluding the KORUS FTA on April 1, 2007, the United States secured nearly complete access for all U.S. agricultural commodities and food products into South Korea's market. However, a breakthrough on the beef issue (technically not part of the FTA talks but nevertheless the subject of high-level discussions) did not occur until June 2008. This reflected the then newly elected Korean President Lee's view that an agreement spelling out the rules that apply to beef imports from the United States had to be in place before President Bush would consider sending this agreement to Capitol Hill. Several Members of Congress had for months stated that South Korea must agree to fully reopen its market to U.S. beef under scientifically based international rules and in commercially significant quantities before Congress considers or approves the agreement. U.S. agricultural groups, well aware of this deal's potential benefits for producers, had then also conditioned their support on the resumption of U.S. beef exports.

Negotiations in late 2010 to address outstanding FTA issues did not result in the full opening of South Korea's market to U.S. beef as sought by the Obama Administration and some Members of Congress. The only change made to the agreement's agricultural provisions is a concession (among others) requested by South Korea in return for changes sought by USTR in the auto provisions. The United States accepted a two-year extension in the phasing out of South Korea's tariff on the largest category of pork imports from the United States. Responding to the conclusion of these talks, the U.S. beef and pork sectors expressed their support for the KORUS FTA, emphasizing that its approval as soon as possible is vital to realizing the gains negotiated before other countries' FTAs with South Korea take effect.

In 2012, South Korea was the fifth-largest market for U.S. agriculture, as export sales totaled $6.0 billion. Under the KORUS FTA's agricultural provisions, South Korea immediately granted duty-free status to almost two-thirds of current U.S. agricultural exports. Tariffs and tariff-rate quotas (TRQs)[26] on most other agricultural goods will be phased out within 10 years (i.e., 2021), with a few commodities and food products subject to provisions that phase out such protection in year 23 (i.e., 2034). Seven U.S. products (skim and whole milk powders, evaporated milk, in-season oranges, potatoes for table use, honey, and identity-preserved soybeans for food use) will be subject to Korean import quotas that slowly expand in perpetuity. However, the agreement does not give U.S. rice and rice products additional access to South Korea's market (see below).[27]

With the immediate elimination or phase-out of most of South Korea's relatively high agricultural trade barriers under the KORUS FTA, the U.S. agricultural and food processing sectors will noticeably benefit from additional exports. The USITC estimates that the increase in U.S. exports of agricultural commodities and processed foods will account for up to one-third of the entire projected increase in total U.S. exports to South Korea's market once the

KORUS FTA's provisions are fully implemented. Sale of agricultural products will increase by $1.9 billion to $3.8 billion (44% to 89%) over exports under a no-agreement scenario. Almost half of this export increase will accrue to the U.S. beef sector, based on the USITC's assumption that U.S. beef exports recover to the level before South Korea imposed its import restrictions in late 2003. About 20% of the export increase will benefit U.S. producers and exporters of pork, poultry and other meat products.[28] In another analysis, the American Farm Bureau Federation (AFBF) projects that U.S. agricultural exports by the end of the transition period will be more than $1.5 billion (45%) higher under the KORUS FTA than would be the case otherwise. Sales of beef, poultry, and pork will account for $644 million (or 42%) of this increase.[29]

Because South Korean agricultural exports to the United States are small ($333 million in2011) and largely complementary, there was no controversy in negotiating access to the U.S. market. The United States agreed to phase out tariffs and quotas on all agricultural imports from South Korea under seven phase-out periods ranging up to 15 years (i.e., 2026). One 10-year TRQ will apply to imports of fluid milk and cream, among other specified dairy products. The USITC projects that imports of agricultural products (primarily processed food products) from South Korea under the KORUS FTA will be from $52 million to $78 million (12% to 18%) higher than such imports under a no-agreement scenario.

Beef

Market Access

Under the KORUS FTA, South Korea agreed to eliminate its 40% tariff on beef muscle meats imported from the United States over a 15-year period. Also, South Korea will have the right to impose safeguard tariffs on a temporary basis in response to any potential surge in imports of U.S. beef meats above specified levels. The trigger for this additional tariff will be 270,000 metric tons (MT) in year 1, which will increase 2% annually; in year 15, the trigger will be 354,000 MT.[30] In year 16, this protective mechanism will no longer apply. The 18% tariff on imports of beef offals (tongues, livers, tails, and feet), and tariffs ranging from 22.5% to 72% on other beef products, will also be eliminated in 15 years.

Assuming that South Korea fully lifts its restrictions on U.S. beef and bilateral beef trade returns to normal, the USITC estimates that the phase-out of South Korea's beef tariff and safeguard could increase U.S. beef exports from about $600 million to almost $1.8 billion (58% to 165%) above what would be the case otherwise. Under the KORUS FTA, the AFBF projects that U.S. beef sales would be $265 million higher as the United States recaptures its historic share of the South Korean market. However, its analysis notes that the market share of U.S. beef likely will not increase over time. That is because South Korean tastes have developed a preference for grass-fed Australian beef, according to the AFBF, and will continue to be competitive in price against U.S. beef even with the current 40% tariff removed.

Sanitary Rules

On April 18, 2008, U.S. and South Korean negotiators agreed to a protocol on the sanitary rules that South Korea will apply to beef imports from the United States. It allows for imports of all cuts of U.S. boneless and bone-in beef and other beef products from cattle, irrespective of age, as long as specified risk materials known to transmit mad cow disease are removed and other conditions are met. However, to address subsequent Korean concerns, both sides revised this agreement on June 21, 2008, to limit sales of U.S. beef from cattle less than 30 months old.

South Korea quickly published rules to put this agreement into effect, and began to inspect U.S. beef shipments. The U.S. Department of Agriculture similarly began to implement a new program to verify that the beef sold is processed from cattle under 30 months old. U.S. beef exporters have since worked to recapture a key overseas market.

In 2003, South Korea was the third-largest market for U.S. beef exports, prior to the ban imposed after the first U.S. cow infected with mad cow disease, or BSE (*bovine spongiform encephalopathy*), was discovered. Korea's commercial significance is reflected in the position taken by some Members of Congress, who had stated that congressional consideration of, and support for, the KORUS FTA depended upon South Korea fully opening its market to U.S. beef.

While the U.S. beef industry and U.S. policymakers welcomed the initial April 2008 deal, Korean TV coverage of the issue and Internet-spread rumors that questioned the safety of U.S. beef resulted in escalating protests and calls for the beef agreement to be renegotiated or scrapped. U.S. officials countered that measures already in place to prevent the introduction of BSE in U.S. cattle herds meet international scientific standards. To address mounting public pressure, the South Korean government twice pursued talks with the United States to find ways to defuse public concerns without "renegotiating" the beef agreement. In late June 2008, both governments confirmed a "voluntary private sector" arrangement that allows South Korean firms to import U.S. beef produced only from cattle less than 30 months old. Both viewed this as a transitional step until Korean consumers regain confidence in the safety of U.S. beef.

Under this arrangement, exports of U.S. beef (including bone-in cuts) to South Korea resumed in mid-2008, and by year-end reached almost $300 million, more than one-third of the record 2003 sales level. In 2009, with the drop off in beef sales worldwide due to the economic recession, U.S. beef sales to South Korea fell to $216 million. For 2010, sales more than doubled to reach $518 million, and then rose further in 2011 to $686 million. Though Australia is the main competitor, U.S. beef exporters have gained noticeable market share since the South Korean market reopened. The U.S. share (in quantity terms) rose from 15% in 2008, 26% in 2009, 32% in 2010, and 37% in 2011 (compared to 69% in 2003). Promotional efforts to rebuild consumer confidence in U.S. beef, aggressive marketing efforts by large store chains, and much lower retail prices for foreign than for Korean beef, account for the continued growth in U.S. beef sales in Korea.[31]

Obama Administration officials, following the President's June 26, 2010, announcement of his decision to present the KORUS FTA to Congress, stated their intent was to resolve the beef and auto issues with South Korea by November 2010 once consultations with Congress and stakeholders were complete. In the negotiations concluded on December 3, 2010, the beef issue reportedly received little discussion as both sides focused on revising the auto provisions. President Obama, in discussing the supplemental agreement, indicated that the United States will continue to work toward "ensuring full access for U.S. beef to the Korean market."[32]

Congressional reaction on the outcome of the beef issue was mixed. Senator Baucus (chairman of the Senate Finance Committee), who had advocated for full access for U.S. beef irrespective of the age of cattle in accordance with international scientific standards, expressed "deep disappointment" that the supplemental deal "fails to address Korea's significant barriers to American beef exports." He stated his commitment to right "this wrong" and to work with the Administration to ensure that ranchers "are not left behind." At that time, Senator Baucus said he will not support the KORUS FTA until South Korea opens up its beef market. A few other Senators, though concerned with the lack of progress on beef, viewed the deal positively and welcomed the prospect for considering the KORUS FTA in 2011.[33] Meat industry groups expressed support for this trade agreement that they expect over time will significantly increase their exports to South Korea, and urged Congress to move quickly to ratify it. Beef interests, also supportive, called for continued efforts to secure full market access.[34]

Memories of the size and intensity of the 2008 anti-beef agreement protests in South Korea appeared to have directly influenced the position then taken on the beef issue by Korean negotiators. Reflecting this political sensitivity, they reportedly rejected any discussion on this matter in the negotiations held in early November 2010 leading up to the summit between Presidents Obama and Lee and in the final talks leading to the supplemental agreement. Their position was that this issue "did not fall under" the FTA concluded in 2007. Subsequently, South Korea's trade minister confirmed that there will be no more discussions on ending the age limits of U.S. cattle slaughtered for beef—a stance that was affirmed by its ambassador to Washington in late January 2011.[35] The outcome appeared to have been successful in that it did not alter the political debate expected to occur in South Korea on the KORUS FTA. However, if changes had been made to the terms of current U.S. beef access, opponents would have been given another opening to shift the debate on the agreement.

Seeking to move closer toward submitting the KORUS FTA to Congress for consideration, the USTR on May 4, 2011, announced two measures to be taken on the U.S. beef access issue. In a letter to Senator Baucus, the Administration committed to request consultations with South Korea on the "full implementation" (e.g., opening Korea's market "to all ages and all cuts of U.S. beef") of the protocol as soon as this trade agreement takes effect. The letter referenced one specific provision that stipulates bilateral consultations on the interpretation or application of the protocol's terms "shall be held within seven days" of a request. On the same day, the U.S. Department of Agriculture (USDA) announced a $1 million award to the U.S. Meat Export Federation (USMEF) to be used in FY2011 to promote U.S. beef sales in South Korea, and its intent to consider future funding requests from the USMEF to implement its planned five-year market beef promotion strategy in this key market. Senator Baucus welcomed both steps, stating he will support the KORUS FTA and work with the Administration on a package of trade measures that includes all three FTAs and renewing trade adjustment assistance and trade preference programs.[36] The KORUS FTA entered into force, but the USTR has not yet had formal consultations with South Korea on the beef issue.

Rice

South Korean negotiators succeeded in excluding the entry of U.S. rice on preferential terms—its prime objective in negotiating agriculture in the KORUS FTA. This reflects Korea's efforts to maintain its stated policy of self-sufficiency in rice production, the national sentiment that preserving rice production is inseparable from the country's identity, and the political reality that rice farming preserves the basis for economic activity in the countryside. That rice was a makeor-break issue for Seoul is seen in the comment made by then-Deputy United States Trade Representative Karan Bhatia, the day after the talks concluded: "Ultimately, the question that confronted us was whether to accept a very, very good albeit less perfect agreement or to lose the entire agreement because South Korea refused to move on rice."[37] On rice, the KORUS FTA only requires South Korea to continue to abide by its multilateral trade commitments to increase rice imports.

At present, U.S. rice exporters have access to the South Korean market under (1) a 24% share (50,076 MT) of the rice import quota established under that country's multilateral World Trade Organization (WTO) commitments in 1995, and (2) a separate "global" quota available to all countries.[38] Rice entering under both quotas faces a 5% tariff. Entries above each quota are prohibited—a unique concession that South Korea received in the 1993 Uruguay Round of multilateral trade negotiations. U.S. rice exports against both quotas have fluctuated much from year to year, and in2011 peaked at $125 million (162,291MT). Future U.S. sales are expected to grow slowly in line with the expansion of the "global" rice quota.

Though the U.S. rice industry expressed disappointment with the rice exclusion, the United States will have other opportunities to negotiate access for additional U.S. rice in Korea's market. A further opening of the South Korean rice market could occur in the process of concluding a multilateral agreement to further liberalize agricultural trade in the WTO's Doha Development Round. Also, the United States and other rice exporting countries could press for additional access when Korea's current WTO minimum market access agreement expires in 2014.

Oranges

Differences on how quickly to liberalize trade in fresh oranges were not resolved until just before the negotiations concluded. The United States sought the complete elimination of South Korea's border protection on all citrus products, while South Korea wanted to retain its quotas and tariffs, primarily because of the importance of the citrus industry to the economy of Cheju

Island. At present, South Korea imposes a 50% tariff on all imports of oranges, irrespective of whether they enter within or outside an existing TRQ.

In reaching a compromise, negotiators agreed to a multi-part solution. First, a small duty-free quota will be created for "in-season" U.S. navel oranges (a variety that is not produced in Korea) that would enter between September 1 and the end of February—a period that coincides with the Island's *unshu* (mandarin) orange harvest season. The initial 2,500 MT TRQ will increase at a compound 3% annual rate in perpetuity. Shipments in excess of the quota amount during this six-month period will continue to be subject to the 50% tariff. Second, in the first year, this high tariff will be reduced to 30% for "out-of-season" oranges that enter between March 1 and August 31, and then be completely phased out in stages by year 7. Third, South Korea's 144% tariff on other mandarin oranges will be phased out over 15 years.

The cost of selling to what already is a leading U.S. export market for fresh oranges will be significantly reduced as Korea's high 50% tariff is phased out. In 2012, South Korea ranked as the leading market, with U.S. orange and tangerine sales totaling $217 million (184,545 MT). The USDA estimates that the value of the in-season 2,500 MT quota and tariff reductions on all orange exports in the first year that the agreement is in effect will be almost $18 million. Over seven years, USDA estimates the cumulative value of savings associated with these orange access provisions at $208 million.[39]

Pork

According to the December 2010 modifications to the initial agreement, South Korea will phase out its 25% tariff on one tariff line of frozen pork cuts on January 1, 2016. This change will affect about 75% of all U.S. pork exports, as recorded by 2010 value. This is two years later than what both sides had agreed upon in the 2007 text (i.e., January 1, 2014). Korea's tariffs on other U.S. pork products will be phased out by January 1, 2014, or over 10 years. South Korea secured a safeguard to protect against import surges of some of these fresh pork products, which will expire at the end of 10 years.

In 2010, South Korea ranked as the fifth-largest market for U.S. pork (fresh, chilled and frozen), with sales of 148,626 MT valued at $433 million. The National Pork Producers Council acknowledged that, even with the last minute concession on pork in order to resolve the auto issue, the KORUS FTA is "a good deal." It expects the agreement to "be one of the most lucrative for the U.S. pork industry," with a substantial increase projected in exports to South Korea, live hog prices, and direct jobs.[40]

Geographical Indications for Dairy Products

The U.S. dairy sector in late 2010 expressed concern that the geographical indications (GI) provisions that apply to various EU cheeses in the KOREU FTA would undercut the potential benefits negotiated under the KORUS FTA for U.S. cheeses with identical names that sell into the Korean market. GIs (similar to a trademark) refer to marks that "identify a good as originating in the territory of a country, or a region or locality in that territory, where a given quality, reputation or other characteristic of the good is essentially attributable to its geographical origin."[41] To illustrate, "champagne" and "Idaho potatoes" are examples of GI designations. Products so designated are eligible for relief from acts of infringement and/or unfair competition under a country's trademark laws and regulations. Because GIs are commercially valuable in the international trade of agricultural products, wines, and spirits, the EU in negotiating its bilateral trade agreements has sought to secure additional protection for its GI-designated agricultural and beverage products in FTA-partner country markets beyond what multilateral trading rules currently provide.

More than 50 Members of the House requested the USTR to ensure that as South Korea develops regulations to implement the KOREU FTA's GI provisions, those rules "do not undercut the dairy market gains secured" in the KORUS FTA. They expressed concern that the U.S. dairy industry will not be able to increase cheese exports if the United States (1) does not "combat European efforts to carve out the sole right for their producers to use ... cheese names most familiar to consumers around the world (e.g., feta, gorgonzola, muenster, parmesan, provolone)," and (2) act to safeguard against possible threats to the use of such generic terms as cheddar and mozzarella "that could arise as a result of recent EU legal precedents" to protect the names of some EU wines and spirits.

A June 2011 exchange of letters between the USTR and Korea's trade ministry clarified that the use of generic terms used to identify types of cheeses (e.g., camembert, mozzarella, emmental, grana, parmesan, brie, cheddar) will not be restricted by the Korea-EU FTA. In other words, U.S. exporters will be able to sell these cheeses into the important South Korean market. A U.S. trade official stated the United States is satisfied with the clarifications provided by South Korea's trade minister. U.S. milk and dairy product groups welcomed these assurances, noting that Korea already is one of the largest export markets for U.S. cheese.[42]

Sanitary and Phytosanitary Provisions

As found in most other U.S. FTAs, the KORUS FTA establishes a bilateral standing committee to address food safety and animal/plant life or health issues that frequently emerge in agricultural trade. However, the agreement does not include any commodity-specific sanitary and phytosanitary (SPS) provisions to address outstanding issues, such as Korea's import health requirements on U.S. beef imports or Korean standards that have prevented sales of some U.S. horticultural products to that market. The Committee on SPS Matters will serve as a forum to implement the WTO's Agreement on the Application of SPS Measures, enhance mutual understanding of each country's SPS rules, resolve future bilateral SPS disputes that arise, coordinate technical assistance programs, and consult on issues and positions in the WTO and other international bodies where SPS issues are considered. The text of the SPS chapter specifically states that neither the United States nor South Korea has recourse to pursue dispute settlement to address any SPS issue that arises. Instead, any matter will be resolved using the formal process established under the WTO's SPS Agreement.

U.S. beef producers had argued until the 2008 bilateral agreement was reached that Korea's stance on U.S. beef imports must be scientifically based upon internationally recognized guidelines issued by the World Organization for Animal Health, also known as OIE by its French acronym.[43] Other agricultural groups also have raised concerns about Korea's implementation of SPS measures on food additives and those that have restricted U.S. fruit and vegetable exports. This new standing committee potentially could be used as the venue to attempt to resolve future SPS disputes, taking into account latest available scientific findings and knowledge.

Automobiles

The final KORUS FTA modified the initial commitments on trade in automobiles in December 2010 and subsequently in an exchange of legal texts on February 10, 2011.[44] The Obama Administration claimed this was a necessary step in approval of the agreement because "the [original] U.S.-Korea trade agreement did not go far enough to provide new market access to U.S. auto companies and to level the playing field for U.S. auto manufacturers and workers."[45] The main components of the KORUS FTA specifically related to automotive trade include:

- *Elimination of South Korean tariffs on U.S.-made motor vehicles.* South Korea has reduced its 8% tariff on U.S.-built passenger cars, including electric vehicles and plug-in hybrids, to 4% and likewise has removed its 10% tariff on trucks.[46] Tariffs on U.S.-made motor vehicles, including electric cars and plug-in hybrids, will be phased out entirely in 2016.[47] In addition, each country dropped its duties to zero on virtually all auto parts imported from the other in 2012.[48]
- Elimination of U.S. tariffs on South Korean-made automobiles and a "snapback" clause. The United States will keep its passenger vehicle rate of 2.5% until the end of 2015. U.S. electric and fuel cell vehicle tariffs dropped to 2% in 2012 and will be reduced annually until duty free in 2016. The 25% duty on trucks, a residual rate dating from an earlier trade dispute with Europe, will stay in place through 2018 and will be duty-free beginning in 2022.49 The FTA, in Annex 22- A, also establishes a special bilateral dispute settlement panel, designed to resolve automotive issues within six months. If the panel finds a violation of an auto-related commitment or the nullification/impairment of expected benefits, the complaining Party may suspend its tariff concessions on passenger vehicles and assess duties at the prevailing MFN rate (i.e., 'snapback' any tariff reductions provided by the FTA)."[50] The final agreement does not extend the snapback to the higher 25% U.S. truck tariff. But measures affecting trucks could lead to the snapback of the 2.5% passenger car tariff. [51]
- *Reduction of alleged discriminatory effects of engine displacement taxes.* Automotive-specific taxes play an important role in determining the final price of a vehicle. U.S. automakers have complained that South Korea's steeply ascending vehicle tax schedule, with very high rates on vehicles with larger engine capacities that might be exported by U.S. producers, makes U.S. imported cars more expensive than smaller South Korean cars. Moreover, the tax system has a "cascade" effect, so that subsequent taxation rates also incorporate the duty paid on an imported vehicle. A special consumption tax, an educational tax, a value-added tax, a registration tax, and a subway bond are currently among the taxes that apply to motor vehicles. As part of the KORUS FTA, the Korean government agreed to simplify and reduce the taxes imposed on each category of passenger vehicles. They also agreed to eliminate the discrepancy in the rates between imported and domestic vehicles by

reducing the tax rate for vehicles in the largest engine-displacement-size categories.[52]

- Improved regulatory transparency for new automotive regulations. South Korea also committed to an improvement in its regulatory process. U.S. auto companies will be given one year between the time a final regulation relating to autos is issued and when U.S. automakers must comply with the new regulation. In addition, South Korea agreed to develop a new post-implementation review system within two years after the agreement takes effect to ensure that existing auto regulations are applied in the least burdensome manner possible.
- *Regulations on harmonization of automotive safety and environmental standards.* U.S. manufacturers have long complained that South Korea sets automotive safety and environmental regulations in a closed and non-transparent manner. This results in standards idiosyncratic to South Korea. As one remedy, the KORUS FTA provides for self-certification to U.S. federal safety standards for a limited number of U.S.-exported vehicles raising the ceiling to 25,000 per automaker per year.[53] Further, the agreement permits some flexibility in meeting new, higher South Korean environmental standards.[54] U.S. automakers will be considered in compliance with new South Korean fuel economy or greenhouse gas emissions standards if "they meet a target level that is 19% more lenient than the relevant target level provided in the regulation that would otherwise be applicable to that manufacturer."[55] This provision applies to U.S. carmakers that sold fewer than 4,500 cars in South Korea in calendar year 2009.
- *Creation of an "Automotive Working Group."* The KORUS FTA established an Automotive Working Group, which should meet at least annually, and will review and resolve "issues with respect to developing, implementing, and enforcing relevant standards, technical regulations, and conformity assessment procedures."[56]
- *Inclusion of a Special Motor Vehicle Safeguard.* The KORUS FTA includes a special safeguard for motor vehicles to ensure that the U.S. auto industry is not hurt owing to any "harmful surges" in South Korea auto imports. The new auto-specific safeguard provision allows the United States to impose extra duties if there is an import surge due to the trade agreement. Any higher tariff that might be imposed could be applied for four years. In the case of truck tariffs, the auto safeguard could be in place until 2031 as it is allowed to continue for

> 10 years after the full elimination of tariffs. Another feature of the safeguard is that it can be applied to a particular auto product more than once in the event of a recurring surge that causes serious injury to U.S. production of that product. It appears easier to apply the safeguard if there are complaints because, as a White House fact sheet notes, "fewer procedural steps are required to speed up the application of the safeguard when workers need faster relief."[57]

The KORUS FTA will not affect the hundreds of thousands of cars assembled by South Korean automakers in the United States and their U.S. production capacity is poised to grow. Thus, a surge in automobile imports from South Korea seems unlikely in the next few years. GM Korea,[58] the South Korean arm of U.S. automaker GM, has manufactured over 100,000 cars in South Korea every year since 2005. See **Appendix** for an overview of South Korea's motor vehicle manufacturing industry.

The USITC simulation model of the KORUS FTA estimates that while U.S. automotive exports to South Korea will increase by a range of 45% to 59%, this will only amount to about $300 million-$400 million because of the low current baseline.[59] It states that tariff elimination "would likely have a positive effect on U.S. exports ... further, the overall tax burden on the South Korean consumer who purchases an imported vehicle would be reduced, more or less equalizing the total taxes paid on imported and domestic vehicles."[60] It particularly emphasizes the potential gain for U.S.-exported hybrid vehicles to South Korea. Whether this will eventually happen remains uncertain. Most hybrids in the U.S. market today are imported from Japan.[61] The Toyota Prius, accounted for more than half, or 136,500, of all hybrid electric vehicles sold in the United States in 2011. Hyundai's Sonata hybrid, the first South Korean hybrid sold in the United States, represented 7% of all such vehicles sold in 2011 to become the second best-selling gas-electric in the United States. Combined, the Detroit-based U.S. manufacturers have increased their hybrid electric vehicle sales in recent years, rising from 0 in 2003 to around 40,000 in 2011. [62]

Alongside hybrids, Hyundai and Kia seem to be considering the development of pickup trucks that could be sold in the U.S. market, although whether they will be produced, and where (in the United States or South Korea), in the near future remains unclear.[63] Hyundai and Kia do already produce small pickup-type vehicles in South Korea, but they would not appear to be suitable in design or style for the United States.[64]

Textiles and Apparel

Textiles and apparel are a small and dwindling portion of U.S. manufactured imports from South Korea. Their respective shares of the U.S. market have fallen in relative and absolute terms. South Korea provided 3% of textiles imported by the United States in 2012, compared with 10% in 1990. Purchases of garments by the United States from South Korea dropped to less than 1% of all apparel imports in 2012, from 10% in 1990. This decrease is largely the result of the surge in U.S. apparel imports from China, which accounted for nearly 40% of all U.S. apparel imports in 2012, from 14% in 1990. The United States exports small volumes of textiles and apparel to South Korea—about $260 million and less than $100 million in 2012, respectively.[65]

The KORUS FTA eliminated U.S. tariffs immediately on 52% (in terms of value) of U.S. imports of South Korean textiles and apparel, and will phase out U.S. tariffs on 19% by 2016 and on the remaining 21% by the end of 2021.[66] Currently, the average U.S. MFN tariff on textiles is 7.9% with a maximum applied tariff of 42%. The average applied U.S. MFN tariff on apparel imports is 11.7% with a maximum tariff of 32%.[67]

The KORUS FTA eliminates South Korean tariffs on 77% (by value) of U.S. exports of textiles and apparel in 2012, then will phase out tariffs on 13% over the next three years and the remaining 10% by 2016.[68] The average South Korean applied tariff on textiles is 9.1% with a maximum of 13%. South Korean tariffs on apparel range from 8% to 13%[69]

The KORUS FTA, with some exceptions, uses the yarn-forward rule of origin for apparel imports; that is, apparel made from yarn or fabric originating in either the United States or South Korea would be eligible for duty-free treatment under the FTA. Also included is a special safeguard provision whereby, if imports of textiles or garments to one KORUS FTA partner country from the other increases at such a rate as to cause or threaten to cause serious injury to the domestic industry of the importing country, the importing country can suspend further reduction of tariffs, or it can increase the duty on the imported product to (the lesser of) the MFN rate applicable at the time the action was taken or the MFN duty that was in force when the FTA went into effect. The safeguard action can be in place for two years with a possible extension of two years, but no more than a total of four years. However, the importing country will have to compensate the exporting country by making additional trade liberalizing concessions equivalent in value to the additional duties expected to result from the safeguard action. The concessions will be limited to textiles and apparel unless the two countries agree otherwise.

The USITC has estimated that the KORUS FTA will over time lead to an increase in U.S. imports of South Korean textiles of $1.7 billion to $1.8 billion and of apparel of $1 billion to $1.2 billion, with the major portion of the increase being diverted from other countries. The USITC also has estimated that the KORUS FTA will lead to an increase in U.S. exports of textiles of $130 million to $140 million and of apparel of $39 million to $45 million to South Korea.[70]

The KORUS FTA will allow some fibers, yarns, and fabrics originating outside the United States and South Korea to become eligible for preferential treatment if the product is not available domestically in commercial quantities in either country. The agreement also provides for the establishment of a Committee on Textile and Apparel Trade Matters to raise concerns under the FTA regarding mutual trade in these products. Absent is a cumulation-specific rule, which, in other trade preference programs and FTAs, allows preferential treatment for limited amounts of apparel woven from components outside the FTA area.

Other Manufactured Goods

Beyond the automotive sector and textiles and apparel, the KORUS FTA affects a wide range of other industries.

Capital Goods Machinery and Equipment

U.S. machinery exports could be the largest single sectoral gainer from the KORUS FTA. According to the USITC's simulation analysis, the sector stands to gain nearly $3 billion in exports of products such as U.S.-made computer-numerically controlled machine tools.[71] The tariffs on U.S. machinery and equipment imported into South Korea range from 3% to 13%, but U.S. products are often competitive and the United States runs an annual trade surplus in machinery products. Most machinery tariffs have been eliminated; others will be phased out between 2014 and 2021.[72] Already duty-free before the implementation of the KORUS FTA, aircraft is another major capital goods item in which the United States has a strong bilateral trade position. U.S. exports to South Korea of aircraft products and parts totaled $3.6 billion in 2012.[73] The U.S. Commercial Service reports that Korea is the 11th largest market for U.S. aerospace exports. Recently, South Korea has embarked on making its aerospace sector more competitive. It intends to raise domestic aerospace production to $20 billion by 2020 from $2 billion in 2009, to establish a strong aircraft production industry to supply Boeing, EADS-Airbus, and to support maintenance of both commercial and military aircraft.[74]

Electronic Products and Components

Because they are parties to the multilateral Information Technology Agreement eliminating tariffs among more than 70 countries, South Korean and U.S. tariffs on most electronics products including semiconductors, telecommunications equipment, and computers were duty-free before the implementation of the KORUS FTA. The few remaining tariffs on U.S. electronics exports such as radio and television parts, certain static converters, and certain telecommunications apparatus—most of which were at 8% prior to March 15, 2012—will be eliminated as of 2014. In 2012, the United States ran a trade deficit in computer and electronic products with South Korea of $6.4 billion, compared with $10.4 billion in 2011. The U.S. trade deficit with South Korea in semiconductors and other electronic components totaled $410 million in 2012, dropping from a record high of $3 billion in 2010.[75] Besides tariffs, the KORUS FTA can provide improvements for U.S. products in South Korea with respect to intellectual property protection, technical barriers, government procurement, and competition policy.[76]

Steel

Steel products represent a significant share of trade between the United States and South Korea. In 2012, South Korea was the 6th largest U.S. export partner in steel products and the 5th largest source of overseas steel imports.[77] South Korea's steel industry is a global player and includes South Korean Pohang Iron and Steel Company (POSCO), the fourth-largest steel producer in the world. The United States ran a record high steel products trade deficit with South Korea of $2.7 billion in 2012.

The American steel industry registered a strongly negative position on the KORUS FTA, raising various objections related to trade remedies, rules of origin provisions, the treatment of products being produced in the Kaesong Industrial Complex of North Korea, and concerns about currency manipulation issues. The specific details of the trade remedies chapter and Kaesong are discussed elsewhere in this report.

Pharmaceuticals and Medical Devices

While pharmaceuticals and medical devices (P&M) are a relatively small part of U.S.-South Korean trade, they are products in which U.S. producers compete well in the South Korean market and ones in which manufacturers see increasing export opportunities as the South Korean economy matures. For years, the U.S. industry and government have complained about a number of South Korea's pharmaceutical policies that allegedly are designed to protect South Korean industry, which predominately produces generic drugs.

South Korea is among the world's top 12 largest markets for pharmaceuticals, accounting for about $8 billion in sales annually.[78] The South Korean market for medical devices accounts for roughly $2.5 billion in sales annually and is expected to grow 10%-15% each year in the next several years, in part due to the rapid aging of the population.[79] While potentially lucrative, South Korea is a market in which U.S. P&M manufactures claim government regulations have limited their ability to penetrate that market.

In 2010, the United States exported $538 million in medical equipment and supplies to South Korea, accounting for 2.1% of total U.S. exports of those products and 1.7% of total U.S. manufactured exports to South Korea. In 2010, the United States exported $825 million in pharmaceuticals and medicines to South Korea accounting for 1.7% of total U.S. exports of pharmaceuticals and 2.1% of total U.S. merchandise exports to South Korea.[80] In the same year South Korea exported $197.3 million in medical equipment and supplies and $80.9 million in pharmaceuticals to the United States.

Of major concern was the South Korean government's May 2006 change in how it determined reimbursement amounts. Prior to the change, it maintained a "negative list" system, under which products would be eligible for reimbursement unless they appeared on the list. With the change, the South Korean government switched to a "positive list" requiring a product to be listed before it would be eligible making it potentially more difficult for a product to become eligible. Announcement of the policy came without prior notification to U.S. officials or affected U.S. manufacturers and occurred at an early point in the negotiations placing a cloud over them. Despite complaints from the United States, South Korea went ahead with implementing its positive list system.

P&M manufacturers also have cited the South Korean government's policies on reimbursements for pharmaceuticals and medical devices under its single-payer health insurance program. U.S. manufacturers have argued that the policies discriminate against innovative pharmaceuticals because they establish relatively low reimbursement amounts for medicines thus not taking into account the costs that producers of leading-edge pharmaceuticals incur and that are reflected in higher prices. The manufacturers wanted the KORUS FTA to establish transparency as an important principal in South Korea's development and implementation of pricing and reimbursement policies, including an appeal process for decisions going against U.S. manufacturers.

In response, South Korea agreed in the KORUS FTA to allow U.S. pharmaceutical makers to apply for increased reimbursement levels based on safety and efficacy. South Korea also agreed to publish proposed laws, regulations, and procedures that apply to the pricing, reimbursement, and regulation of pharmaceuticals and medical devices in a nationally available publication and to allow time for comment. In addition, South Korea agreed to establish a process for U.S. manufacturers to comment on proposed changes in laws and regulations and for them to obtain a review of administrative determinations that adversely affect them. However, the Pharmaceuticals Research and Manufacturers of America (PhRMA) has not fully implemented its commitments. USTR indicated that it is working with the South Korean to establish a date for the first meeting of the binational Medicines Committee to resolve outstanding issues.[81]

Intellectual property rights protection in South Korea has been a critical issue for U.S. pharmaceutical manufacturers. Specifically, the failure of the South Korean government to protect from competitors proprietary data that manufacturers must submit for market approval. In addition, the South Korean government has, in some cases, approved marketing of some pharmaceuticals before it has determined that the applicant is the rightful owner of the patent and trademark.[82]

In response, under the KORUS FTA's data exclusivity provisions, South Korea would not allow a third company, such as a generic drug manufacturer, from marketing a new pharmaceutical using the safety and efficacy data, supplied by an original U.S. manufacturer as part of the market approval process, without the permission of the original U.S. maker for five years from the date of marketing approval for the original product. In addition, if a third party submits safety or efficacy information for a product that an FTA partner government had already approved, the government is to notify the original patent holder of the identity of the third party and is to prevent the marketing of the third party's product on its territory if permission had not been granted by the original patent holder. In a side letter, the United States and South Korea originally agreed to not invoke the data exclusivity provision until the FTA has been in effect 18 months. Under the modifications to the commitments, the United States agreed to double to 36 months, or three years, the time South Korea will have to put in place a system of patent linkages for pharmaceuticals that is required under the FTA. Furthermore, South Korea agreed to a patent-linkage system; that is, neither government is to approve the marketing of a generic drug while the original patent is still in effect. Another provision, known as patent-term extension, would require each FTA government to adjust the length of the effective period for patents on pharmaceuticals to take into account delays incurred in receiving patent approval and marketing approval. The KORUS FTA states that no provision would prevent either government from taking measures to protect the public health of its residents from HIV/AID, tuberculosis, malaria, and other epidemics, by ensuring access to medicines. The FTA would reaffirm each country's commitment to the WTO TRIPS/health Declaration.

Reactions within the pharmaceutical and medical devices industries were somewhat split on the KORUS FTA. Makers of innovative products supported the provisions that are designed to preserve the rights of patent holders and provisions that are designed to make the South Korean regulatory, pricing, and reimbursement process more transparent and open to comments and procedural reviews. At the same time, industry representatives remained critical of South Korea's new reimbursement procedures and argued that the new system does not take into account the benefits of innovative drugs that cause drug prices to be higher. Generic drug manufacturers argue that the KORUS FTA does not contain provisions guaranteeing the availability of affordable drugs.[83] While pharmaceuticals and medical devices (P&M) are a relatively small part of U.S.-South Korean trade, they are products in which U.S. producers compete well in the South Korean market. U.S. manufacturers also see increasing export opportunities as the South Korean economy matures. For years, the U.S. industry and government have complained about a number of South Korea's pharmaceutical policies that allegedly are designed to protect South Korean industry, which predominately produces generic drugs.

Overseas sales are critical to the U.S. pharmaceutical industry; some U.S. multinational firms generate revenues of 40% or higher in foreign markets.[84] South Korea is the 5th largest market in Asia, with pharmaceutical sales at an estimated $15.4 billion in 2011. By 2016, its market is projected to grow to around $24 billion.[85] Although South Korea's pharmaceutical sector is the fast-growing developed country market, according to IMS Healthcare, it currently represents less than 2% of the global pharmaceutical market.[86]

South Korea is also an important market for U.S. medical equipment and device manufacturers valued at an estimated $3.7 billion in 2011[87] and could grow 10%-15% each year in the next several years, partly due to a rapidly aging population.[88] While potentially lucrative, South Korea is a market in which U.S. P&M manufactures claim government regulations have limited their ability to penetrate that market.

The United States sold $995 million in pharmaceuticals and medicines to South Korea in 2012, representing around 2% of all U.S. exports of pharmaceuticals to South Korea.[89] Exports of medical equipment and supplies to South Korea totaled $525 million in 2012, accounting for less than 2% of total U.S. exports of medical equipment to South Korea. In the same year, the United States ran trade surpluses with South Korea in both pharmaceuticals and medical equipment and supplies.

Of major concern during the KORUS FTA negotiations was the South Korean government's May 2006 change in how it determined reimbursement amounts. Prior to the change, it maintained a "negative list" system, under which products would be eligible for reimbursement unless they appeared on the list. With the change, the South Korean government switched to a "positive list" requiring a product to be listed before it would be eligible making it potentially more difficult for a product to become eligible. Announcement of the policy came without prior notification to U.S. officials or affected U.S. manufacturers and occurred at an early point in the negotiations placing a cloud over them. Despite complaints from the United States, South Korea went ahead with implementing its positive list system.

P&M manufacturers also cited the South Korean government's policies on reimbursements for pharmaceuticals and medical devices under its single-payer health insurance program. U.S. manufacturers argued that the policies discriminate against innovative pharmaceuticals because they establish relatively low reimbursement amounts for medicines thus not taking into account the costs that producers of leading-edge pharmaceuticals incur and that are reflected in higher prices. U.S. manufacturers wanted the KORUS FTA to establish transparency as an important principal in South Korea's development and implementation of pricing and reimbursement policies, including an appeal process for decisions going against U.S. manufacturers.

In response to these concerns, South Korea agreed in the KORUS FTA to allow U.S. pharmaceutical makers to apply for increased reimbursement levels based on safety and efficacy. South Korea also agreed to publish proposed laws, regulations, and procedures that apply to the pricing, reimbursement, and regulation of pharmaceuticals and medical devices in a nationally available publication and to allow time for comment. In addition, South Korea agreed to establish a process for U.S. manufacturers to comment on proposed changes in laws and regulations and for them to obtain a review of administrative determinations that adversely affect them. Intellectual property rights protection in South Korea has been a critical issue for U.S. pharmaceutical manufacturers. Specifically, the failure of the South Korean government to protect from competitors proprietary data that manufacturers must submit for market approval. In addition, the South Korean government has, in some cases, approved marketing of some pharmaceuticals before it has determined that the applicant is the rightful owner of the patent and trademark.[90]

In response, under the KORUS FTA's data exclusivity provisions, South Korea will not allow a third company, such as a generic drug manufacturer, from marketing a new pharmaceutical using the safety and efficacy data, supplied by an original U.S. manufacturer as part of the market approval process, without the permission of the original U.S. maker for five years from the date of marketing approval for the original product. In addition, if a third party submits safety or efficacy information for a product that an FTA partner government had already approved, the government is to notify the original patent holder of the identity of the third party and is to prevent the marketing of the third party's product on its territory if permission had not been granted by the original patent holder. In a side letter, the United States and South Korea originally agreed to not invoke the data exclusivity provision until the FTA has been in effect 18 months. Under the modifications to the commitments, the United States agreed to double to 36 months, or three years, the time South Korea will have to put in place a system of patent linkages for pharmaceuticals that is required under the FTA. Furthermore, South Korea agreed to a patent-linkage system; that is, neither government is to approve the marketing of a generic drug while the original patent is still in effect. Another provision, known as patent-term extension, requires the United States and South Korea to adjust the length of the effective period for patents on pharmaceuticals to take into account delays incurred in receiving patent approval and marketing approval. The KORUS FTA states that no provision would prevent either government from taking measures to protect the public health of its residents from HIV/AID, tuberculosis, malaria, and other epidemics, by ensuring access to medicines. The FTA reaffirms each country's commitment to the WTO TRIPS/health Declaration.

Financial and Other Services

U.S. service providers exported $16.8 billion in services to South Korea in 2011. Among them were South Koreans' travel to the United States ($3.8 billion); other transportation, such as freight services ($2.1 billion); royalties and license fees ($4.5 billion); and other private services, such as professional services, business services, banking, insurance, and other financial services ($6.1 billion).[91] However, this amount probably undervalues the total volume of U.S. sales of services to South Korea as services are also sold through three other modes of delivery: by U.S. companies with a long-term presence in South Korea, by U.S. providers to South Korean residents located temporarily in the United States, and by U.S. providers temporarily located in South Korea.

In 2011, the United States imported $11.0 billion in services, including other transportation ($2.4 billion), U.S. travel to South Korea ($1.7 billion), expenditures by U.S. military ($2.6 billion), and other travel ($1.7 billion).[92] This figure does not include services sold to U.S. residents by South Korean firms through the other modes of delivery.

U.S.-South Korean trade in services cuts across several chapters of the KORUS FTA—Chapter 12 (cross-border trade in services); chapter 13 (financial services); and Chapter 15 (telecommunications); chapter 11 (foreign investment); among others. A major U.S. objective in the KORUS FTA negotiations was to obtain South Korean commitments to reduce barriers to trade and investment in its services sector, especially in professional, financial, and telecommunications services.

In general the two countries committed to:

- provide national treatment and most-favored-nation treatment to the services imports from each other;
- promote transparency in the development and implementation of regulations in services providing timely notice of decisions on government permission to sell services;
- prohibit limits on market access, such as a caps on the number of service providers, on the total value of services provided, on the total quantity of services provided, and on the total number of persons that can be employed by services providers;
- prohibit foreign direct investment requirements, such as export and local content requirements and employment mandates; and
- prohibit restrictions on the type of business entity through which a service provider could provide a service.

U.S. and South Korean negotiators agreed to several concepts under the KORUS FTA that could apply the agreements' provisions to a broad scope of services. The two countries agreed to the "negative list" approach in making commitments in services. That is, the KORUS FTA is to apply to all types of services unless identified as an exception in the relevant annexes. In addition, the commitments are ratcheted—when new services emerge in the U.S. or South Korean economies, those services are automatically covered by the FTA unless identified as an exception; if either country unilaterally liberalizes a measure that it had listed as an exemption, it is automatically covered under the FTA. Furthermore, if one KORUS FTA partner extends preferential treatment to service providers from a third country under another FTA, it is to extend the preferential treatment to its KORUS FTA partner.

The United States sought greater reciprocity in the treatment of *professional services* and thereby gain increased access to the South Korean market for U.S. providers. The United States and South Korea agreed to form a professional services working group to develop methods to recognize mutual standards and criteria for the licensing of professional service providers. Under the KORUS FTA, South Korea will allow U.S. law firms and U.S. licensed attorneys to provide advisory services on U.S. and international law on entry into force of the KORUS FTA. South Korea will also permit U.S. legal representative offices to establish cooperative operations with a South Korean firm to handle matters pertaining to domestic and foreign legal matters, and, no later than five years after the agreement's entry into force, will allow U.S. law firms to form joint ventures with South Korean firms. However, South Korea will still reserve the right to restrict the activities of foreign lawyers.

Regarding *financial services*, under the KORUS FTA, if a domestic provider in one partner country develops and sells a new financial service in its home market, providers from the FTA partner country will be able to sell a like service in that market. The agreement will allow an FTA partner government to impose restrictions on the sale of financial services by providers from the other partner country for prudential reasons, for example, to protect investors, depositors, policy holders, or persons to whom a fiduciary duty is owed. The FTA will also permit either partner government to restrict monetary transfers in order to ensure the soundness of financial institutions.

The South Korean *insurance* market is the seventh-largest in the world. The USITC estimates, therefore, that U.S. insurers will be poised to obtain sizeable gains in a liberalized South Korean services market.[93] U.S. insurance companies have been concerned that the state-owned Korea Post and the cooperative insurance providers—the National Agricultural Cooperative Federation and the National Federation of Fisheries Cooperative—are not regulated by the Korean Financial Supervisory Commission or by the Financial Supervisory Service, while both private-sector foreign and domestic providers are so regulated.[94] Under the KORUS FTA, South Korea agreed that those entities will be subject to an independent state regulator as opposed to being selfregulated.[95] In addition, Korea Post will not be allowed to offer new insurance products. The two countries will allow a partner country financial services provider to transfer electronically information from its territory as necessary in the course of doing business.[96] This is a provision that the U.S. industry highlighted as being particularly important.

In *telecommunications services*, South Korea will reduce government restrictions on foreign ownership of South Korean telecommunications companies. Two years after the KORUS FTA enters into force, U.S. companies will be able to own up to 100% of voting shares in domestic South Korean telecommunications companies, and those companies will be able to own up to 100% of a facilities-based licensee.[97] These provisions do not apply to KT Corporation nor to SK Telecom Co for which a 49% foreign ownership limit will remain. In addition, each KORUS FTA partner will ensure that telecommunications providers from the other would have access to and use of its public telecommunications network for purposes of interconnection under nondiscriminatory conditions and will guarantee dialing portability among other conditions.[98]

Those who represent U.S. services providers were enthusiastic about the KORUS FTA and urged its approval. In a statement, Robert Vastine, then-president of the Coalition of Services Industries claimed:

> We commend Ambassador Schwab and the team of negotiators who secured significant benefits for U.S. services providers in this agreement.... Korea is a key market for U.S. service companies, and this is a very high-quality agreement that merits swift passage by the Congress because it creates new commercial opportunities that will support new jobs.[99]

Visas

For years, a priority for South Korea has been to convince the United States to ease restrictions on the issuance of visas for South Korean business representatives. The visa issue—along with South Korea's request to be added to the Visa Waiver program (VWP), which allows visa free travel for short-term visitors—was addressed in discussions outside of the KORUS FTA negotiations. On October 17, 2008, President Bush announced that South Korea was one of seven countries that would be admitted into the program in 4-6 weeks.[100] With this step, the VWP is likely to no longer be an issue in bilateral relations. South Korea is one of the United States' largest sources of foreign visitors. In FY2007 there were 811,251 short-term visitors for business or pleasure from South Korea.[101]

On a separate track, as part of the package of modifications agreed to on December 3, 2010, the United States agreed to extend the initial validity period of L-1A visas for South Korean nationals. These visas are used by foreigners entering the United States to work at U.S.-subsidiary of a foreign company. One group of these visas are used for foreigners coming to establish a U.S. subsidiary and the initial validity period was extended from one to five years. A second group is used for foreigners coming to work at an already established subsidiary and the initial validity period was extended from three to five years.[102]

GENERAL PROVISIONS

The KORUS FTA text contains a number of provisions that cut across in many sectors in bilateral trade. Many of these provisions have become standard fare and have become part of the template for FTAs in which the United States participates.

Trade Remedies[103]

Trade remedies, laws, and actions designed to provide relief to domestic industries that have been injured or threatened with injury by imports, are regarded by many in Congress as an important trade policy tool to mitigate the adverse effects of lower priced imports on U.S. industries and workers.

The three most commonly used trade remedies are *antidumping* (AD), *countervailing duty* (CVD), and *safeguard* actions. Antidumping (19 U.S.C. §1673 *et seq.*) actions provide relief from the adverse impact of imports sold at prices shown to be less than fair market value, and countervailing duty (19 U.S.C. §1671 *et seq.*) actions provide similar relief from goods that have been subsidized by a foreign government or other public entity. Safeguard actions (19 U.S.C. §2251 *et seq.*) are designed to give domestic industries an opportunity to adjust to new competition and are triggered by import surges of fairly traded goods. The relief provided in a safeguard case is a temporary import duty, temporary import quota, or a combination of both, while the relief in an antidumping or countervailing duty action is an additional duty placed on the dumped or subsidized imports. These actions are authorized by the WTO as long as they are consistent with the rights and obligations of Article XIX of the General Agreement on Tariffs and Trade (GATT) 1994, the WTO Agreement on Safeguards and Countervailing Measures (Subsidies Agreement), and the WTO Agreement on Implementation of Article VI of the GATT 1994 (Antidumping Agreement).[104]

Many Members of Congress have expressed support for maintaining and strengthening U.S. trade remedy laws in the face of growing import competition. As a result, the preservation of U.S. authority to "enforce rigorously its trade laws" was a principal negotiating objective included in presidential Trade Promotion Authority (TPA) in the 107th Congress.[105]

According to news reports, the "single most important South Korean demand" in the bilateral talks was changes to U.S. antidumping rules.[106] This may be due, in part, to the significant number of U.S. trade remedy cases brought by U.S. industries on South Korean goods. As of February 12, 2010, antidumping duties were being collected on 12 South Korean imports (mostly on stainless steel specialty products such wire rod and pipe fittings), and countervailing duties were being assessed on 3 South Korean products, while South Korea had no trade remedy measures in place against U.S. products.[107] The U.S. global safeguard cases imposed on steel in February 2000 (line pipe) and March 2002 (many steel products) also significantly reduced South Korean steel imports to the United States.[108] Of the 14 WTO dispute resolution complainant cases South Korea has brought to date, 8 have been disputes against U.S. trade remedy actions.[109] South Korea is also a member "Friends of Antidumping" group in the WTO Doha Round that insists on implementing changes to the Antidumping and Subsidies Agreements in any new multilateral agreement.

In the bilateral negotiations between the United States and South Korea, talks broke down in early December 2006 when South Korea presented the United States with a list of specific changes to U.S. antidumping laws on a "basically" take-it-or-leave-it basis,[110] but in mid-January 2007, South Korean officials softened their stance after accepting the assurances of U.S. negotiators that Trade Promotion Authority had granted the Bush Administration only limited flexibility to make concessions on trade remedy issues.[111]

The KORUS FTA, just as in earlier FTAs the United States has entered into, indicates that each party to the agreement will retain all rights and obligations under the WTO agreements—meaning that the trading partners will be permitted to include each other in global safeguard actions (although, as in other FTAs, it does extend a possible exemption from global safeguard measures to either party if its imports are not a substantial cause of serious injury) and to implement AD and CVD actions against each other. Additionally, as in earlier FTAs, the trade remedies article also authorizes either party to the agreement to apply a transitional safeguard measure against imports of the other party if, as the result of the reduction or elimination of a duty mandated by the agreement, a product is being imported in increased quantities as to be a substantial cause of serious injury to a domestic industry that produces a like or directly competitive good.[112]

In the case of a safeguard, the party imposing it must provide a mutually agreed-upon amount of compensation. If the parties do not agree, the other party may suspend concessions on imports of the other party in an amount that has trade effects substantially equivalent to the safeguard measure.[113]

As such, the agreement does not require any changes to U.S. AD or CVD laws, or regulations. However, in an apparent departure from previous FTAs, the KORUS FTA seems to require a few additional administrative steps prior to initiation of a trade remedy investigation involving goods from the other party. First, each party will have to notify the other if an antidumping petition is received regarding the other party's imports, as well as provide an opportunity for a meeting between the parties before an investigation is initiated.[114] Additionally, the party initiating an AD or CVD investigation will be required to provide written information regarding its procedures for negotiating a price or quantity undertaking (known in U.S. law as a suspension agreement),[115] and, after a preliminary affirmative determination is reached, "provide due consideration and adequate opportunity for consultations regarding proposed price undertakings" which could result in suspension of the investigation without imposition of duties provided a mutually agreeable undertaking is reached.[116]

The KORUS FTA will also establish a Committee on Trade Remedies (which is to meet at least once a year) made up of representatives from each party who has responsibility for trade remedies matters. Committee functions include enhancing knowledge of the parties' trade remedy laws and practices, overseeing the implementation of the trade remedies chapter of the agreement, improving cooperation between the parties, developing educational programs on trade remedy laws, and providing a forum for exchange of information on trade remedies and other topics of mutual interest.[117]

As discussed earlier, the Industry Trade Advisory Committee on Steel (ITAC 12) believes that the procedural concessions made on trade remedies could politicize trade remedy actions, thus possibly weakening U.S. trade laws. In particular, the ITAC 12 stated that the U.S. AD-CVD investigative process is already transparent and that the pre-initiation notification and consultation requirements will delay and politicize the process.[118] It also objected to the "undertakings" provisions, saying that these provisions will encourage the use of suspension agreements and introduce actions of foreign governments into trade remedy procedures.[119] (For more information on the steel industry's reaction, see discussion in section on "Other Manufactured Goods.)

The ITAC 12 also opposed the establishment of a Committee on Trade Remedies, saying that it such a forum will give South Korea an opportunity to attempt to further try to weaken U.S. trade remedy laws.[120] Speaking in April 2007, Assistant U.S. Trade Representative for Korea, Japan, and APEC Wendy Cutler, the chief U.S. negotiator, implied that the consultative committee will focus on information sharing and "will not provide a forum to discuss specific cases."[121] She also mentioned that the committee could be a benefit to the United States by providing a platform for discussing certain industrial subsidies that the South Korean government may be supplying to manufacturing firms, and that negotiators worked out an "accommodation" that was beneficial to both sides' needs on a very contentious part of the negotiations.[122]

Kaesong Industrial Complex[123]

A consistent and significant goal for South Korea in the FTA talks was securing preferential treatment for products made in the Kaesong Industrial Complex (KIC) in North Korea, a position the United States adamantly opposed throughout most of the negotiations. Located near the North Korean city of Kaesong (also spelled "Gaesong"), 40 miles north of Seoul, the KIC is designed for South Korean companies to employ North Korean workers. As of the end of 2010, over 120 medium-sized South Korean companies were employing over 47,000 North Korean workers to manufacture products in Kaesong. The facility, which in 2010 produced $323 million in output, has the land and infrastructure to house two to three times as many firms and workers. Products vary widely, and include clothing and textiles (71 firms), kitchen utensils (4 firms), auto parts (4 firms), semiconductor parts (2 firms), and toner cartridges (1 firm).

The KIC has generated controversy because it provides an ongoing revenue stream to the Kim Jong-il regime in Pyongyang, by virtue of the share the government takes from the salaries paid to North Korean workers. South

Korean and U.S. officials estimate this revenue stream to be around $20 million per year. On the other hand, the KIC arguably helps maintain stability on the Peninsula and provides a possible beachhead for market reforms in the DPRK that could eventually spill over to areas outside the park and expose tens of thousands of North Koreans to outside influences, market-oriented businesses, and incentives.

In the final KORUS FTA agreement, the two sides reached a compromise on the KIC. On the one hand, the agreement does not include any reference to the complex, and KIC products are not eligible for the agreement's special treatment provisions.[124] On the other hand, a binational committee will be formed to study the possibility of eventually incorporating products from "Outward Processing Zones" (OPZs), including those—like the KIC—that are located in North Korea.[125] The agreement identifies three general categories for which the committee is to develop more detailed criteria: progress in the denuclearization of North Korea, developments in intraKorean relations; and wages, business management practices, the environment, and labor standards. For the third category of issues, the committee is to consider relevant international norms as well as the "situation prevailing elsewhere on the Peninsula." After the committee has developed criteria, the OPZ provisions in the FTA lay out a three- step process by which products made in the KIC could be incorporated into the FTA. First, the committee must deem that an outward processing zone meets the criteria it has established. Second, the two governments must agree that the FTA should be amended accordingly. Third, both governments must seek "legislative approval for any amendments to the Agreement with respect to outward processing zones." The agreement does not lay out the size or composition of the committee, or how committee members will be chosen, or the procedures by which the committee is to arrive at decisions, except that decisions would have to be reached by unified consent.[126]

For years, neither the Bush nor Obama Administrations specified what form "legislative approval" for OPZ-related amendments to the KORUS FTA would take. In March 2011, the office of the United States Trade Representative (USTR) issued a statement that Congress "would need to pass, and the President would need to sign, a law to extend any KORUS FTA tariff benefits to products made in Kaesong or any OPZ."[127]

Some observers, particularly many opponents of the KORUS FTA, argued that the agreement could lead to increased U.S. imports of goods or components made in North Korea. The scenario they suggest involves South Korean firms obtaining low-cost Kaesong-made goods or components, incorporating the latter into finished products such as electronics or automobiles, and then reshipping the goods to the United States with "Made in [South] Korea" labels. If the KORUS FTA were in effect, the argument runs, these goods might receive preferential treatment. However, a close analysis of the agreement and the nature of trade flows reveals that unless the KIC is brought into the KORUS FTA, the FTA would likely have only a marginal impact on whether the United States imports North Korean finished products or goods that contain North Korean components. Instead, the extent of the problem of North Korea imports will be largely determined by the degree to which North Korean producers become integrated into the global economy. In addition, imports from North Korea require U.S. government approval. This restriction includes finished goods originating in North Korea as well as goods that contain North Korea-made components.

Another criticism of the KORUS FTA was that it could constrain the United States' ability to restrict imports of North Korean goods or components, for instance, by invoking the agreement's dispute settlement procedures to challenge a U.S. decision to prohibit the entry of a South Korean product that contains North Korean components. However, provisions in the KORUS-FTA will appear to allow either the United States or South Korea to impose or maintain trade restrictions against the goods of a third country (such as North Korea); thus the agreement will accord each Party the right to restrict trade with the other Party in implementing any such embargo.

In the KORUS FTA negotiations, the United States backed away from the principle of its initial position of not ever expanding the KORUS FTA to North Korea-made products, a significant achievement for South Korea. At the same time, the United States appeared to give up little in substance in the near-to-middle term. The United States apparently would be able to control the decision to and pace of any move to grant preferential treatment to North Korea-made products. Any perceptions of foot-dragging by the United States, however, may come at a diplomatic price if future South Korean governments push for more rapid integration of North Korean industrial zones into the FTA.

Foreign Investment

Foreign investment is becoming an increasingly significant element in the U.S.-South Korean bilateral economic relationship. Over the past decade, the stock of U.S.-South Korean foreign direct investment (FDI), valued on an historical cost basis, has increased substantially, due in no small part to the market-oriented reforms South Korea undertook after its 1997 financial crisis. In 1997, the value of stock of U.S. FDI in South Korea was $6.5 billion and had increased to $31.8 billion by the end of 2011 (latest data available). South Korean FDI in the United States has also increased substantially, albeit from a much lower base. In 1997, the stock of South Korean FDI in the United States was valued at $0.6 billion and had increased to $18.4 billion by the end of 2011 (latest data available).[128]

Foreign investment has been a sensitive issue in U.S.-South Korean relations for many years as U.S. investors have tried to make inroads into the South Korean economy. U.S. investors' criticisms have included restrictions on foreign investment in key sectors, such as communications, and the lack of adequate protection for intellectual property. (See section on "Intellectual Property Rights.") Efforts to establish bilateral rules have failed in the past. In the 1990s, the two countries tried to negotiate a bilateral investment treaty (BIT), that would commit each party to provide national treatment to the investments from the other party and abstain from performance requirements for foreign investments from the other party. But the negotiations collapsed largely over U.S opposition to South Korea's so-called screen quota on domestic films and the latter's resistance to lifting or reducing it. (The South Korean government reduced the screen quotas by half just before the KORUS FTA negotiations were launched in February 2006.) The KORUS FTA chapter on investment essentially contains the commitments that would otherwise have been in a BIT.

The FTA sets down general principles for the treatment by South Korea and the United States of investors and investments from one partner in the territory of the other.[129] The principle of national treatment—that one party to the agreement will treat covered investments and investors from the other party no-less favorably than it treats domestic investors and investments—is paramount. The FTA allows each party to make exceptions to the national treatment principle, but those exceptions must be specified in the relevant annexes to the agreement.[130] A second fundamental principal is most-favored-nation treatment (MFN)—the two parties agree to treat investors and investments from the other no less favorably than it treats investors and investments from third, non-party countries. A third principle is minimum standard of treatment, that is, each party shall accord to all covered investments treatment in accordance with customary international law, including fair and equitable treatment and full protection and security.

The KORUS FTA sets limits on government expropriation of covered investments—that they be only for public purpose and carried out in a nondiscriminatory manner, and affected investors will be provided with prompt and adequate compensation (fair market value). It also requires each KORUS FTA partner-country government allow for the free transfer of financial capital pertaining to covered investments both into and out of the country with exceptions, such as cases related to criminal offenses. The KORUS FTA prohibits the U.S. and South Korean governments from imposing performance requirements (domestic content requirements, export-ratios, import limits, etc.) on the investments from the other. It will allow exceptions for measures intended to accomplish social objectives, such as to increase employment in certain regions of the country, promote training of workforce, and protect the environment. The agreement also prohibits a requirement that senior managers be of a particular nationality but will allow a requirement that the majority of board of directors be of a particular nationality.

Similar to other U.S. FTAs, the KORUS FTA establishes procedures for the settlement of investor-state disputes involving investments covered under the agreement where the investor from one partner-country alleges that the government of the other partner-country is violating his rights under the FTA. The FTA stipulates that the two parties should try to first resolve the dispute through consultations and negotiations. But, if that does not work, the agreement provides for arbitration procedures and the establishment of tribunals as provided under the "Convention on the Settlement of Investment Disputes Between States and Nationals of Other States."

The USITC concluded that U.S. investors, especially investors in financial services, would likely gain from the KORUS FTA.[131] (See section on "Financial and Other Services.") The United States has been the predominate partner in terms of foreign investment and stands to gain the most from the protections provided by the KORUS FTA. However, South Korean investments in the United States are increasing, and therefore, South Korea could benefit as well.

Intellectual Property Rights

In addition to those sections addressing pharmaceutical manufacturing (see discussion above), the KORUS FTA contains other provisions on intellectual property rights (IPR) protection in U.S.- South Korean trade. Under the FTA the United States and South Korea reaffirm their commitments under the WTO Trade-Related Aspects of Intellectual Property Rights (TRIPS) agreement and other international agreements and conventions on intellectual property. But the two countries made IPR commitments beyond those agreements with provisions that

- require each government to extend national treatment to IPR holders from the other country;[132]
- require transparency through the publication of regulations and laws regarding intellectual property rights;
- facilitate the registration of and protection of trademarks and established limitations on the use of geographical indications;
- ensure the right of authors, performers, producers of recordings to determine use of copyrighted products;
- require copyright protection for no less than 70 years; thus, South Korea agrees to extend its copyright protection term, an objective of U.S. copyright holders;
- protect copyrighted material against piracy and provide penalties for those who abet piracy including the seizure and destruction of pirated and counterfeit products;
- protect copyrighted performances on the internet; and
- protect encrypted programming over satellites and cable signals.

Labor Rights and Conditions

On May 10, 2007, a bipartisan group of congressional leaders and the Bush Administration released a statement that provided language to be included in pending FTAs, including KORUS FTA. Among other things, the statement, or framework, called "The New Trade Policy for America," requires U.S. FTA partners to commit to enforcing the five basic international labor standards and would require that the commitment be enforceable under the FTA.[133] Neither country is to waive or otherwise derogate from its labor statutes that reflect the five labor rights in a manner that affects trade or investment between the two FTA countries. Each country is to ensure that those affected by their respective labor laws have access to tribunals that enforce their rights under those laws. During his nomination process, USTR Ron Kirk stated the Obama Administration's position that the KORUS FTA appropriately incorporates the May 10th understanding.[134]

Under the KORUS FTA the two countries are to form a Labor Affairs Council made up of officials from the respective labor ministries and agencies, that is to meet within the first year after the agreement enters into force. At least one session of the council will be devoted to meeting with the public in each country to discuss matters related to the enforcement of the labor provisions of the FTA. Disputes regarding labor matters under the FTA are to be resolved first by consultations, but if those fail, the parties in dispute may take the matter to the Labor Council and eventually to a dispute settlement panel if these mechanisms fail to resolve the dispute. The KORUS FTA also calls for the establishment of a Labor Cooperation Mechanism whereby the two countries would develop and work in areas pertaining to labor rights in each country.

To many outside observers, South Korea's labor rights regime is generally considered to be strong for regular workers. South Korea ranks in the top third of the OECD's thirty members in terms of employment protection for regular workers.[135] Indeed, for years, a major complaint of U.S. multinationals is that restrictions in the South Korean labor market, such as mandatory severance pay, significantly raise the cost of investing and doing business in Korea. In contrast, U.S. union representatives argue that recent changes to make South Korean labor markets more flexible are reducing the rights of South Korean workers.[136] Korea's unions have earned a reputation for activism; the number of working days lost to strikes is regularly among the highest in the OECD. Hyundai Motors, for instance, has experienced a strike every year since 1994. Moreover, strikes in South Korea are notable in that they are sometimes accompanied by violence and the occupation of workplaces and public spaces (such as highways), to which the government often responds with police action. In its comments on the KORUS FTA, the Labor Advisory Committee for Trade Negotiations and Trade Policy (LAC), criticized South Korea for the imprisonment of around 200 unionists who were "exercising basic labor rights" and for mobilizing riot police against union activity.[137]

Korea's labor pool is divided into two segments: (1) South Korean "salarymen" (salaried workers, overwhelmingly men, in large corporations) comprise less than one-third of the workforce. Over half of this segment of the workforce is represented by powerful unions. (2) The remainder of the workforce is comprised of employees in small-scale firms plus the country's temporary and day laborers. Few of these workers are unionized. The proportion of temporary workers has grown markedly, to nearly one-third of the workforce, one of the highest rates in the industrialized world.[138] These workers tend to receive low wages and receive limited coverage by the social safety net, points highlighted by the LAC. Labor markets are notoriously rigid.

Government Procurement

A great deal of business is conducted by governments through the purchase of goods and services for their own use. Most governments, including the United States have laws (The Buy American Act) which require such goods and services to be of domestic origin. However, the General Agreement on Tariffs and Trade (GATT) and now the WTO have some provisions, the WTO Government Procurement Agreement (GPA), under which the countries agree to open up some of their government procurement business, to foreign companies as a way to promote trade. This agreement is plurilateral, that is it only applies to those WTO members that have signed it. The United States and South Korea are among the 41 signatories to the GPA. The GPA established rules for governments to publish information about contract tenders, including technical specification, about qualification for suppliers, the awarding of contracts, with a specific emphasis on nondiscrimination and transparency in the conduct of government procurement.

The KORUS FTA reaffirms the GPA as a baseline for government procurement but would expand the criteria to include more contracts. The GPA applies to contracts valued at around $203,000 and above. The KORUS FTA applies to contracts valued at $100,000 and above, potentially increasing the value of bilateral government-procurement trade. The GPA applies only to contracts tendered by 79 U.S. federal government agencies and by 42 South Korean central and subcentral agencies listed in the annex. Under the KORUS FTA, South Korea add ed nine more agencies to be covered.

Environment Protection

In keeping with the May 10, 2007, understanding on labor and the environment between the Bush Administration and congressional leaders, under the KORUS FTA, the United States and South Korea commit to enforce a list of seven multilateral environmental agreements to which both are parties and to add to the list when other agreements enter into force. (See the "Labor Rights and Conditions" section above.)[139] In addition, the FTA will prevent the two countries from easing environmental standards in order to allow firms on their territory from gaining a competitive trade advantage. Furthermore, violations of the environmental provisions are to be handled in the same manner as commercial provisions through the dispute settlement mechanism of the KORUS FTA and subject to trade sanctions, unprecedented for U.S. FTAs. As mentioned earlier, the Obama Administration has indicated that the May 10, 2007 agreement is incorporated into the KORUS FTA.[140]

Transparency

Making information publically available is a fundamental principle imbedded in international trade rules and in each of the FTAs that the United States has entered into. For years U.S. exporters and trade negotiators identified the lack of transparency of South Korea's trading and regulatory systems as one of the most significant barriers to trade with South Korea, in almost every major product sector. Under KORUS FTA, the United States and South Korea commit: to publish relevant regulations and administrative decisions as well as proposed regulations; to allow persons from the other party to make comments and to ask questions regarding proposed regulations; to notify such persons of administrative proceedings and to allow them make presentations before final administrative action is taken; and to allow such persons to request review and appeal of administrative decisions.

Institutional Provisions and Dispute Settlement

The KORUS FTA provides several options for the United States and South Korea to resolve disputes arising under the agreement, in addition to the special dispute settlement provisions under the foreign investment chapter and other chapters. KORUS FTA requires the two countries to establish a joint committee chaired by the USTR and the Minister of Foreign Trade or their designees to supervise the implementation of the agreement. The trade agreement provides for the establishment of a panel to adjudicate disputes between the two countries under the agreement, if consultations do not lead to a resolution of the dispute. Annex 22A of the KORUS FTA contains provisions for the settlement of disputes regarding motor vehicles, specifically the snap-back provision. (See discussion in section on "Automobiles") Annex 22-B provides for eventual discussion of the inclusion of products made in outward processing zones in North Korea. (For more information, see discussion in "Kaesong Industrial Complex" section.)

Other Technical Provisions

The KORUS FTA includes other sets of provisions intended to facilitate market access. *Technical barriers to trade* are standards and regulations that are intended ostensibly to protect the health and safety of consumers and for other legitimate non-trade purposes but may through design and implementation discriminate against imports. The KORUS FTA commits both countries to uphold their obligations under the WTO Agreement on Technical Barriers to Trade (TBT). In addition, South Korea and the United States will promote transparency, by allowing persons from the other party to participate in the development of standards, technical regulations, and conformity assessment procedures.

Regarding *customs administration and trade facilitation,* the KORUS FTA will promote joint cooperation to ensure compliance with each other's customs laws and regulations. For example, it requires the two countries to adopt procedures and regulations to facilitate express delivery shipments.

Rules of origin define what are goods that originate in the FTA region and therefore are eligible for preferential treatment. (Textiles and apparel have separate rules of origin.) The KORUS FTA will require that goods must be wholly obtained or produced in the territory of both countries or country. The FTA sets a regional value threshold to be met to be considered originating in the FTA territory and provides formulas for determining the regional values.

National *competition laws and regulations* are intended to ensure that one firm does not so dominate a sector of the economy as to inhibit market entry and stifle competition. Among other things, the KORUS FTA requires that the United States and South Korea inform persons, who are subject to administrative actions, of hearings and provide them the opportunity to make their case. The two countries will cooperate in enforcing competition laws through the exchange of information and consultation. In addition, designated monopolies and state-enterprises will have to operate in conformance with the agreement and in accordance with commercial considerations.

The KORUS FTA includes provisions to facilitate trade via electronic commerce (*e-commerce*). They prohibit discrimination against digital products and imposing customs duties on these products. They also require the recognition of electronic authentication and electronic signatures and would promote consumer access to the Internet.

LEGISLATIVE ACTION

On October 3, 2011, President Obama submitted draft legislation (H.R. 3080/S. 1642) to implement the U.S.-South Korea Free Trade Agreement (KORUS FTA) to both houses of Congress. On October 6, the House Ways and Means Committee reported out H.R. 3080 (H.Rept. 112-239). On October 11, the Senate Finance Committee reported out S. 1642 (S.Rept. 112-223). On October 12, the House passed H.R. 3080 (278-151) and sent it to the Senate which passed it (83-15) later the same day. The President signed the legislation on October 21, 2011 (P.L. 112- 41). The votes on the KORUS FTA implementing legislation took place after the White House and congressional leaders agreed to procedures under which legislation to implement the KORUS FTA and legislation to implement the other two pending FTAs with Colombia and Panama would be considered in tandem with legislation to renew certain aspects of the Trade Adjustment Assistance (TAA) program. An action-forcing event was the October 13, 2011, state visit of South Korean President Lee Myung-bak to Washington.

IMPLICATIONS FOR SOUTH KOREA AND THE U.S.-ROK ALLIANCE

The Ratification Debate

In South Korea, on November 22, 2011, the National Assembly ratified the KORUS FTA and over a dozen implementing bills. The debate over the agreement's ratification was contentious and divisive, despite the fact that President Lee's party, the conservative New Frontier Party (NFP), controls the National Assembly. Korea's largest opposition party, the left-of-center Democratic Party (DP), opposed the agreement. For weeks, it and its allies physically blocked the Assembly's Committee on Foreign Affairs, Trade, and Unification from considering the FTA. Additionally, many NFP leaders were reluctant ram the agreement through the Assembly for fear of repercussions in parliamentary elections scheduled for April 2012. After repeated attempts at negotiations failed to produce a breakthrough, the GNP's leadership on November 22 surprised nearly all observers by calling the full Assembly into a special session for a snap vote on the KORUS FTA and several implementing bills.[141] The National Assembly passed the KORUS FTA by a vote of 151-7, with 12 abstentions. (The Assembly has 299 members.)

South Korea's Opposition Parties Call for Re-Negotiation or Withdrawal

In the months since the vote, politicians from the DP and other left-of-center parties have continued to speak out against the KORUS FTA. In early 2012, the DP and a like-minded group merged to form the Democratic United Party (DUP). Shortly after its formation, senior DUP officials called for renegotiating nine areas of the agreement, including the investor-state dispute settlement mechanism and the 2010 automotive safeguards provisions. The coalition also has stated it wants to change the agreement's rules of origin to allow goods manufactured in the Kaesong Industrial Complex, inside North Korea, to be granted preferential trade status. In multiple fora – including a letter to President Obama, Vice President Joseph Biden, and Speaker of the House John Boehner – the DUP chairwoman, Han Myong-sook, stated that her party would withdraw South Korea from the agreement if it was voted into power and its demands were not met. Subsequently, the DUP softened its stance by calling for a "complete renegotiation" instead of "scrapping" the agreement. The change came after Han and other DUP leaders were criticized for championing the KORUS FTA while they were officials in the previous South Korean government of Roh Moo-hyun, which was in power from 2003-2008.

Upcoming Elections

Even if the DUP takes control of the National Assembly in the April 2012 vote, as a number of observers predict, it would not have the ability to withdraw from the KORUS FTA. The more important election will occur in December 2012, when South Koreans will elect a new president, who would have the power to terminate the agreement. The true significance of the April vote for the KORUS FTA may be as a bellwether: if voters are perceived as rewarding or punishing the DUP for its stance on the agreement, it is likely to determine whether the party's nominee for the presidency makes re-negotiation of or withdrawal from the agreement a priority.

South Korea's Motives for Pursuing the KORUS FTA

Entering an FTA with the United States meshed with a number of Lee's economic and strategic goals. Ongoing competitive pressure from Japanese firms, increased competition from Chinese enterprises, and the rapid aging of the South Korean workforce has heightened the sense of urgency to boost national long-term competitiveness, particularly in the services industries, where South Korean productivity typically lags compared to other industrialized countries. Indeed, former President Roh and other South Korean officials argued that the KORUS FTA is essential for South Korea's economic survival.[142] Similarly, if less grandiosely, President Lee has argued that KORUS FTA will help boost South Korea's economy. To accelerate Korea's reform efforts— and also to avoid being left out from other FTAs being created globally and in Asia—Presidents Roh and Lee have pursued an aggressive effort to negotiate FTAs. South Korea has entered into FTAs with (in order of completion) Chile, Singapore, the European Free Trade Association (EFTA), the Association of Southeast Asian Nations (ASEAN), India, the European Union, Peru, and the United States. It is negotiating FTAs with seven other countries – including Canada, Mexico, and Australia – and officially discussing nine other FTAs, including agreements with China and Japan.[143]

The United States and South Korea negotiated the KORUS FTA in part as a means to restore the health of a critical foreign policy and national security alliance.[144] While the talks were ongoing in 2006 and 2007, the KORUS FTA sometimes was discussed as a possible counterweight to the bilateral friction that was occurring over issues such as how to manage relations with North Korea and the repositioning of U.S. troops in South Korea. These tensions decreased markedly in 2007, following the Bush Administration's decision to place greater emphasis on engagement and negotiations with North Korea. The December 2007 election of Lee, who has stressed the importance of rebuilding U.S.-South Korean ties has improved relations further. Thus, with the alliance on firmer ground, the KORUS FTA no longer appears as an exceptional area of bilateral cooperation.

Although the FTA's utility as an acute salve for the alliance has been reduced, some argue it will help to boost the alliance, over the medium and longer term, by deepening bilateral economic and political ties. Entering into an FTA, some argue, is a way to help reorient the alliance to adapt to the changes on the Korean Peninsula and in East Asia. However, in concrete terms, it is difficult to see how the KORUS FTA would make a significant difference in the strategic relationship, as it is unlikely to alter either country's fundamental interests on the Peninsula or in Northeast Asia.

In contrast, while the *passage* of the KORUS FTA was unlikely to have a major substantive impact on the strategic relationship, a *collapse* of the KORUS FTA would probably have had a profound symbolic effect, particularly upon the way South Koreans view the alliance. If the KORUS FTA had been rejected or subjected to a prolonged delay by the United States, it would have been a psychological blow to many South Korean policymakers, many of whom would likely see it as a betrayal. This would be particularly true since, in their eyes, they made politically costly concessions on autos, beef, labor, and the environment to help ensure the agreement would be more favorably received in the U.S. Congress. The KORUS FTA's failure in the United States, according to some Korean politicians and policymakers, would have lent credence to arguments in South Korea that the U.S. commitment to Korea and Northeast Asia is declining. If these perceptions had taken hold, it would increase the political costs of South Korean leaders' taking unpopular decisions on behalf of the alliance, such as increasing South Korea's share of the costs of maintaining U.S. troops on the Peninsula.

IMPLICATIONS FOR U.S. TRADE POLICY AND U.S. ASIA POLICY

Leading up to the congressional vote on the KORUS FTA, President Obama faced competing pressures. On one side were those, including business community representatives and pro-trade Members of Congress, who viewed the KORUS FTA as an important opportunity for the United States to increase trade and investment with an important East Asian market and ally. They also were concerned about U.S. manufacturers and investors losing out to their EU competitors since the EU-Korea FTA entered into force before the KORUS FTA on July 1, 2011. On another side, were those who argued that the KORUS FTA did not sufficiently address South Korean barriers to imports of manufactured goods, particularly cars and some appliances. The KORUS FTA faced even deeper opposition from those who are skeptical about the benefits of FTAs, in general, at least as pursued under current trade policy.

But the commitment modifications contained in the 2011 exchange of letters appeared to have accomplished their primary objective. They shifted the politics surrounding the KORUS FTA debate in the United States, where the original agreement was encountering strong resistance and without fundamentally altering the politics in South Korea, where the agreement had broad support. Shortly after the announcement, a number of U.S. groups and individuals who had previously opposed the agreement, including several Members of Congress, announced their support. In South Korea, the modifications appeared not to have shifted the terms of political debate over the FTA, which generally had been expected to be approved by the National Assembly. Most South Korean media commentators have observed that the balance of concessions in the December deal were in the United States' favor, a dynamic that the agreement's opponents have seized upon as another reason to criticize the FTA. In contrast, South Korean supporters of the agreement appear to accept the concessions as regrettable but tolerable.

The fate of the KORUS FTA could affect U.S. efforts to institutionalize its economic presence in East Asia. In addition to the KORUS FTA, the United States has an FTA with Singapore. The Bush Administration initiated FTA negotiations with Malaysia and Thailand, but they ultimately stalled. In November 2009, President Obama announced the United States would enter into negotiations on a Trans-Pacific Partnership (TPP) trade agreement, a trade liberalization negotiation among Australia, Brunei Darussalam, Chile, New Zealand, Peru, Singapore and Vietnam. The FTA may become even larger in the coming months. Japan, Canada, and Mexico have begun consultations with these eight countries, plus the United States, over joining the TPP negotiations. President Obama, Secretary of State Hillary Clinton, and other U.S. officials have said that the KORUS FTA, along with the TPP, are key parts of their move to "pivot" U.S. strategic orientation toward the Asia-Pacific region.

U.S. use of FTAs in Asia also has been a proposed response to the plethora of bilateral and multilateral FTAs that are being negotiated in the region. None of the actual or proposed multilateral agreements include the United States. Failure of the KORUS FTA could have been viewed as a serious blow to the U.S. "competitive liberalization" strategy. With FTAs throughout East Asia proliferating, a failure of the KORUS FTA to be implemented would also likely have meant that the United States would be shut out of regional economic groupings in East Asia. In contrast, the implementation of the KORUS FTA could spark interest of other East Asian countries, such as Japan, to negotiate FTAs with the United States in order not to lose their share of the huge U.S. market to South Korea. Thus, if the proponents of the "competitive liberalization" argument are correct, the fate of the KORUS FTA could play an important role in accelerating or decelerating the move to open market regionalism in East Asia. Indeed, in the fall of 2011, the KORUS FTA's supporters in Korea argued that ratification was necessary because of Japan's intention of joining the TPP talks, much as TPP proponents in Japan had used the KORUS FTA as a justification to promote their cause.

Similarly, the fate of the KORUS FTA is likely to be seen as a bellwether for broader U.S. trade policy, which is now in a period of reevaluation. In addition to the KORUS FTA, U.S. FTAs with Colombia and Panama are pending. The Doha Development Agenda round in the WTO is, for all intent and purposes, on life support. This raises questions in the minds of U.S. policymakers and other experts, regarding the future role of the WTO and multilateral negotiations in shaping the international trading framework. The KORUS FTA will likely play a role in this reassessment. For better or worse, its rejection or indefinite delay might call into question the viability of FTAs as a serious U.S. tool to strengthen economic ties with major trading partners.

APPENDIX. SOUTH KOREAN MOTOR VEHICLE MANUFACTURING

South Korea came late to the table of major motor vehicle manufacturing nations. Government attempts to foster a domestic automobile industry began in 1962 when the South Korean government enacted the Automobile Industry Protection Law, with assembly line production of automobiles in Korea beginning that year using complete knock down kits imported from Japan.[145] The 1980 edition of the *Automotive News Market Data Book*, an authoritative industry source, listed no South Korean company among the top 50 global producers. By 2011, according to the International Organization of Motor Vehicle Manufacturers (OICA), total South Korean production of cars and commercial vehicles was given as 4.7 million units; South Korea ranked as the global number five national producer, behind, in order, China, the United States, Japan, and Germany.[146] Yet, South Korea remains only a mid-level consumer of motor vehicles, with domestic sales of 1.4 million in recent years. Exports accounted for 70% of Korea's motor vehicle production volume in 2012, a figure that is matched by no other major motor vehicle producing country.[147]

South Korea has aggressively developed and protected its automotive manufacturing base. Motor vehicle imports were prohibited in South Korea until 1987, and imports from Japan were banned until 1999.[148] Originally the South Korean government promoted the development of a fleet of domestically owned producers, but this strategy failed. In the shakeout after South Korea's economic crisis of 1997-98, only one major South Korean-owned company was left, Hyundai, which also took control of the number-two producer by volume, Kia. Others were marginalized, out of the business altogether, or controlled by foreign companies. Korea's third producer, and their only other major manufacturer left in the business, Daewoo, is now controlled by General Motors.[149] The lone major South Korean-owned producer, the Hyundai-Kia combination, in 2011 produced 6.6 million vehicles worldwide, ranking it fourth globally.[150]

Hyundai is a world-class global competitor, with current and planned assembly operations in the United States, the European Union, and other countries. The export orientation of the South Korean motor vehicle industry, the quality of South Korean cars, and the relatively low U.S. tariff on all imported motor vehicles, except trucks, has made the United States a good market of opportunity for South Korean automobile exports. Until 2016 and 2021, respectively, the United States will impose a 2.5% duty on imported passenger vehicles and a 25% duty on trucks. South Korean auto makers export many more cars to the United States than U.S. car manufacturers export to South Korea. Total South Korean motor vehicle exports to the United States peaked at more than 860,000 units in 2004, according to U.S. Commerce Department data, and have dropped every year through 2009, but increased to more than 700,000 passenger vehicles and light trucks in 2012 (see **Figure A-1**). U.S.-based automobile exporters, which could include South Korean and other foreign-owned manufacturers, shipped more than 22,600 passenger cars and light trucks to South Korea in 2012, compared with nearly 15,000 in 2011.[151]

Another important development affecting automotive exports and imports are the investments South Korean automakers have made in the U.S. market since the mid-2000s. Hyundai and Kia have established production facilities in the United States. Thus, Hyundai's Montgomery, AL, plant and Kia's West Point, GA, facilities allow them to substitute for some imports. In 2012, Hyundai and Kia sold nearly 1.3 million light vehicles in the United States, of which nearly 60%, or about 720,000 units, were produced in the United States.[152] More than 360,000 Hyundai Sonatas and Elantras were assembled in Alabama and about 230,000 Kia Sorento's and Hyundai Santa Fe's were produced in Georgia in 2012.[153] At full capacity, the Georgia Kia plant will be able to produce 300,000 vehicles. Meanwhile, GM Korea, which is the South Korean arm of U.S. automaker GM, builds and sells cars in South Korea. In

2011, GM Korea sold 125,730 domestically built cars.[154] Since these vehicles are not exported they are not covered by the KORUS FTA.

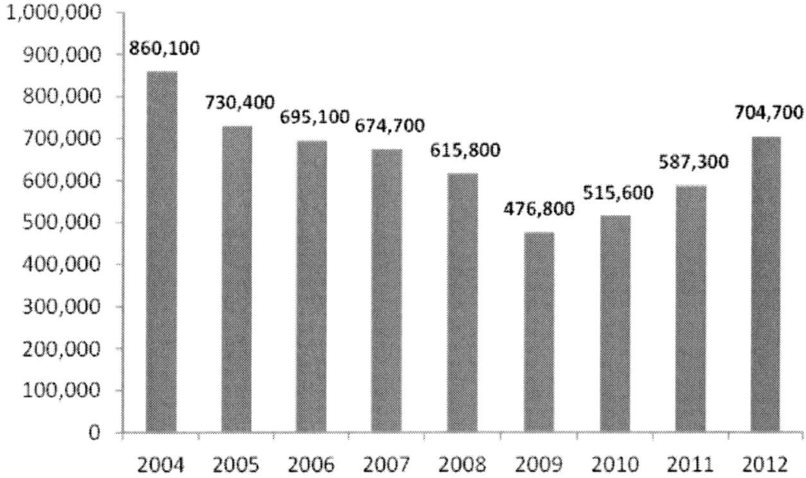

Source: U.S. Department of Commerce, Office of Transportation and Machinery and the American Automotive Policy Council.

Figure A-1. South Korean Passenger Vehicle and Light Truck Exports to the United States; (2004-2012).

The total value of South Korean automotive exports to the United States, including parts, was $18.6 billion in 2012, compared with U.S. exports of similar products to South Korea of $1.3 billion. The United States ran a bilateral trade deficit in autos of $17.3 billion in 2012, which widen from $11.3 billion five years ago.[155] One analyst who examined the effects of the FTA, found in simulation models of projected market changes, South Korea would always gain relative to the United States from bilateral liberalization, "because Korea has a comparative advantage over the United States in the automobile sector; in other words, Korea has been much more successful in accessing the U.S. market than the United States has been in accessing the Korean market."[156]

Through aggressive and successful marketing, Hyundai and Kia together have significantly increased U.S. market share from the 2000s. Both brands saw a jump in their U.S. sales (for Hyundai sales of both their domestic and imported vehicles increased by 9% from 2011 to 2012 and Kia's car and light truck sales rose by 15% during the same time period). By comparison, overall sales of U.S. light vehicles grew to 14.4 million units in 2012 from 12.7 million in 2011, or by 13%. Despite their growth in sales, South Korean automakers share of the U.S. market remained largely unchanged in 2012 over 2011 at around 8.8%, but rose from 7.1% in 2010. Sales of Chevrolet's Aveo model, which is imported from South Korea, dropped to 67 units in 2012 from 28,600 in 2011.[157]

For years, South Korean policies that allegedly restrict imports of foreign-made motor vehicles have been a major target of U.S. trade policy. In 1995 and 1998, the USTR negotiated memoranda of understanding (MOUs) with South Korea, aimed at reducing formal and informal South Korean policies that were said to discriminate against imports of U.S.-made vehicles and other foreign imports. U.S. policy primarily focused on motor vehicle taxation policies and South Korean motor vehicle standards, which supposedly did not conform to international standards, or those widely used in major markets.[158] The import share of the domestic market in South Korea has increased since the MOUs were signed. According to data from the Korea Automobile Manufacturers Association and the Korea Automobile Importers and Dealers Association, total imports grew from a low of less than 1% of the market (4,400 units) in 2000 to 8.5% market share by 2012 (130,900 units). Together, European manufacturers accounted for three-quarters of imported cars in the South Korean market in 2012 and Japanese manufacturers combined comprised another 18%. U.S.-headquartered automakers made up the remainder with a 7.4% share of new imported cars sold in South Korea (i.e., Ford at 5,100, Chrysler at 4,100, and GM at 475).[159]

End Notes

[1] White House Office of the Press Secretary, "Background Readout by Senior Administration Officials to the Travel Pool on the President's Meeting with President Lee Of The Republic Of Korea," April 2, 2009.

[2] *International Trade Daily.* June 17, 2009.

[3] White House Press Release, "Remarks by President Barack Obama and President Lee Myung-Bak of Republic of Korea in Joint Press Conference," November 19, 2009.

[4] "TRANSCRIPT: Fox News Interviews President Obama," FOXNews.com, updated November 18, 2009.

[5] United States International Trade Commission (USITC). *U.S.-Korea Free Trade Agreement: Potential Economy-wide and Selected Sectoral Effects.* Investigation No. TA-2104-24. USITC Publication 3949. September 2007.

[6] For more on the U.S.-South Korean alliance, see CRS Report RL33567, *Korea-U.S. Relations: Issues for Congress*, by Larry A. Niksch.

[7] The December 2010 commitment modifications adjusted the tariff elimination schedule for passenger cars and trucks, a longer phase-out period was a key priority for Ford Motor Company and the United Auto Workers (UAW), added a special vehicle safeguard to protect the U.S. market from a possible surge in South Korean auto imports, and increased the exemption for U.S. car manufacturers from South Korean safety standards if they meet U.S. federal safety standards. U.S. and South Korean trade negotiators signed legal texts, which included these new commitments for the automotive sector, on February 10, 2011.

[8] In the initial 2007 agreement the United States and South Korea had agreed to phase out their respective electric and hybrid car tariffs of 2.5% and 8%, over ten years.

[9] For more information see pp. 2-4 of CRS Report R-41544, *Trade Promotion Authority and the U.S.-South Korea Free Trade Agreement*, by Emily Barbour.

[10] "*U.S. Light Vehicle Sales, December & YTD*," WardsAuto, January 4, 2013, http://www.wardsauto.com and data from the American Automotive Policy Council.

[11] Trade Remedy Piece of Korea FTA Ignores Korean ADF Demands. *Inside U.S. Trade.* April 13, 2007.

[12] §2104(f) Trade of 2002. P.L. 107-210. United States International Trade Commission (USITC). *U.S.-Korea Free Trade Agreement: Potential Economy-wide and Selected Sectoral Effects.* Investigation No. TA-2104-24. USITC Publication 3949. September 2007. (Hereafter referred to as USITC (2007).) In March 2011, the USITC released a study updating its analysis of the KORUS FTA's impact on the U.S. passenger vehicle market as a result of the December 2010 modifications, *U.S.-Korea Free Trade Agreement: Passenger Vehicle Sector Update,* Investigation No. 332-523, USITC Publication 4220, March 2011.

[13] USITC (2007). pp. xvii-xviii.

[14] USITC (2007). p. xix.

[15] Kiyota, Kozo and Robert M. Stern. *Economic Effects of a Korea-U.S. Free Trade Agreement.* Korea Economic Institute, Special Studies 4. 2007.

[16] Lee, Junyu and Hongshik Lee. *Feasibility and Economic Effects of a Korea-U.S. FTA.* Korean Institute for International Economic Policy. December 2005. p. 86.

[17] OECD, *Economic Surveys–Korea*, 2007.

[18] Korea Economic Institute, "Current Economic Info, South Korean Economic Data," at http://www.keia.org, January 2, 2008.

[19] "ROK Editorial: Roh's 'Special Lecture'," *The Korea Times*, posted on the Open Source Center, KPP20060329042002, March 29, 2006.

[20] Ministry of Finance and Economy Weekly Briefing, "Korea-US FTA Projected to Boost the Korean Economy," March 9, 2006.

[21] See, for instance, Junkyu Lee and Hongshik Lee, *Feasibility and Economic Effects of a Korea-U.S. FTA* (Seoul: Korea Institute for International Economic Policy, 2005), pp. 116-117; Inbom Choi and Jeffrey Schott, *Free Trade between Korea and the United States?* (Washington, DC: Institute for International Economics, 2001), pp. 79-82.

[22] "Roh's 'Special Lecture'," *The Korea Times*, March 26, 2006.

[23] Korea Broadcast System, March 31, 2006, Broadcast.

[24] The KORUS FTA Tariff Schedule can be found in the USITC report, *Modifications to the Harmonized Tariff Schedule of the United States to Implement the United States-Korea Free Trade Agreement*, USITC Publication 4308, February 2012, http://www.usitc.gov/publications/tariff_affairs/USITCPub4308.pdf.

[25] South Korea's average applied agricultural tariff in 2010 was 48.6%, compared to 5.0% for the United States, from WTO, "Country Profiles" for South Korea and the United States,

September 2012, available at http://stat.wto.org/CountryProfiles/KR_e.htm and http://stat.wto.org/CountryProfiles/US_e.htm.

[26] A TRQ is a two-part tool used by countries to protect their more sensitive agricultural and food products, often while transitioning over time to free trade. The quota component provides for duty-free access of a specified quantity of a commodity, which in an FTA usually expands over time depending on the outcome of the negotiations. Imports above this quota are subject to a prohibitive tariff that in an FTA may or may not decline over time. At the end of a product's transition period to free trade under an FTA, both the quota and tariff usually no longer apply (unless specific exceptions are made), allowing for its unrestricted access to the partner's market.

[27] Summaries of commodity-specific market access provisions (tariff reduction schedules, transition periods, TRQ amounts and growth rates, and safeguards) are found in the USDA fact sheets "U.S. - Korea Trade Agreement," March 2011, available at http://www.fas.usda.gov/itp/KoreaTA/KORUS%20One-Page%20Fact%20Sheet%2003-11.pdf, and "U.S. Korea Trade Agreement - Benefits for Agriculture," March 2011, available at http://www.fas.usda.gov/itp/KoreaTA/KORUS%20Detailed%20Fact%20Sheet%2003-11.pdf. Detailed fact sheets on the agreement's commodity provisions and prospective impacts for agriculture in 45 states are available at http://www.fas.usda.gov/info/factsheets/Korea/us-korea tafactsheets.asp.

[28] Derived by CRS from Table 2.2 in USITC, *U.S.-Korea Free Trade Agreement: Potential Economy-wide and Selected Sectoral Effects,* Publication 3948, September 2007, pp. 2-8 and 2-9.

[29] Derived by CRS from the AFBF's *Implications of a South Korea-U.S. Free Trade Agreement on U.S. Agriculture*, July 2007, p. 17. To be consistent with the agricultural and food product categories used to derive the USITC's estimate, AFBF's exports of fish products are not included in the estimated increase in agricultural exports and agriculture's share stated above.

[30] In 2003, U.S. exports of beef muscle meats to South Korea totaled 213,083 MT. The safeguard level in year 1 would allow for duty-free access for about 20% more U.S. beef than the average 2002-2003 level of U.S. beef exports to the South Korean market. For comparison to the recent past (in 2012), U.S. beef muscle cut meat exports were 111,991 MT.

[31] For more information, see CRS Report RL34528, *U.S.-South Korea Beef Dispute: Issues and Status*, by Remy Jurenas and Mark E. Manyin.

[32] White House, Office of the Secretary, "Remarks by the President at the Announcement of a U.S.-Korea Free Trade Agreement," December 4, 2010.

[33] Senate Finance Committee, "Baucus Deeply Disappointed With Announcement on Korea Trade Deal, Commits to Keep Fighting for American Ranchers," December 3, 2010; Senate Agriculture Committee, "Sen. Chambliss Statement on U.S.-South Korea Free Trade Agreement," December 3, 2010; Senator Grassley, "Conference Call with Farm Broadcasters," December 7, 2010; *Washington Post*, "Senator's objection may slow trade pact," February 3, 2011, p. A4.

[34] Meatingplace.com, "U.S.-Korea FTA deal leaves beef unchanged, phases out tariffs," December 6, 2010;National Cattlemen's Beef Association, "Statement from NCBA Chief Economist Gregg Doud on US, Korea Trade Deal," December 3, 2010; American Meat Institute, "AMI Statement on Finalized U.S. Free Trade Agreement with South Korea," December 3, 2010.

[35] *Inside U.S. Trade*, "Korean Negotiators Refused To Engage On Beef Issue In Seoul," November 19, 2010; *Washington Trade Daily*, "The KorUS Supplemental Agreement,"

December 6, 2010, p. 3; Washington Post, Political Economy Blog, "Obama, Lee outlined U.S.-Korea trade deal in Seoul, official says," December 6, 2010; Bloomberg, "South Korea's Kim Rules Out Negotiations on U.S. Beef Imports," December 6, 2010; *Inside U.S. Trade*, "Baucus to Oppose Korea FTA Unless More Progress Made on Beef Issue," December 10, 2010, p. 3; International Trade Daily, "Korea Has No Plans to Discuss Beef Prior to Action on FTA, Ambassador Says," February 1, 2011.

[36] Senate Finance Committee, "Baucus Secures Administration's Commitment to Expand U.S. Beef Access in Korea," May 4, 2011, accessed at http://finance.senate.gov/newsroom /chairman/release/?id=51481 3d3-9192-4a38-8f5aea602675f442.

[37] *Inside U.S. Trade*, "USTR Says Beef Market Access Must Precede Signing of Korea FTA," April 6, 2007, p. 5.

[38] Following the 2004 renegotiation of South Korea's WTO agricultural commitments, the United States and most other rice exporting countries beginning in 2005 have been able to take advantage of this separate global quota. Expanding by 20,347 MT each year through 2014, market access is on a first-come, first served basis. By 2014, both rice import quotas (under country allocations made to four countries including the United States, and the quota available to any country) will total 408,700 MT. For background on Korea's market access and domestic policies for rice, see USDA, Economic Research Service, South Korea Briefing page titled "Policy," available at: http://www.ers.usda.gov/topics/international-markets-trade/countries-regions/south-korea/policy.aspx.

[39] USDA, Foreign Agricultural Service, Fact Sheet "U.S.-Korea Free Trade Agreement—What's At Stake for Fresh Citrus and Orange Juice," September 2008.

[40] NPPC, "U.S.-South Korea FTA Remains A Good Deal For U.S. Pork Producers," December 3, 2010.

[41] Uruguay Round Agreement on Trade-Related Aspects of Intellectual Property Rights (TRIPS), Article 22.1.

[42] Letter from Korea's Trade Minister Jong-Hoon Kim to USTR Ron Kirk, June 20, 2011; *Inside U.S. Trade*, South Korea Clarifies GI Provisions in EU-Korea FTA to USTR Satisfaction, June 24, 2011; U.S. Dairy Industry press release, "U.S. Rights to Export Variety of Cheeses to Korea Upheld," June 23, 2011, available at http://www.usdec.org/ files/PressReleases /NMPFUSDECIDFA-U.S.RightstoExportVarietyofCheesestoKoreaUpheld.pdf.

[43] This stance is reflected in testimony by the National Cattlemen's Beef Association before the USITC on June 20, 2007.

[44] USTR, Legal Texts Reflecting December 3, 2010 Agreement, February 10, 2011, http://www.ustr.gov/tradeagreements/free-trade-agreements/korus-fta/legal-texts-reflecting-december-3-2010-agreement.

[45] White House. "*Increasing U.S. Auto Exports and Growing U.S. Auto Jobs Through the U.S.-Korea Trade Agreement*," December 3, 2010, http://www.whitehouse.gov/sites/default/files /fact_sheet_increasing_us_auto_exports_us_korea_free_trade_agreement. pdf.

[46] Tariffs on trucks cover pickup trucks, panel vans, and commercial vehicles. Many light trucks such as SUVs and minivans are counted as cars.

[47] Tariffs for electric cars and plug-in hybrids will phase out between 2012 and 2016, whereas passenger car tariffs will remain at 4% until 2016.

[48] Office of USTR. *KORUS FTA: Opportunities for Automotive Exports* October 2008, http://www.ustr.gov/archive/assets/Document_Library/Fact_Sheets/2008/asset_upload_file500_15206.pdf.

[49] The 2007 agreement would have required the United States to begin phasing out its 25% tariff on light truck imports immediately until full elimination in year 10 following implementation of KORUS FTA.

[50] USTR, "Auto-Related Provisions," p. 1; USITC. *U.S.-Korea FTA*, p. 3-80 (Box 3-4). In the case of the United States the most-favored-nation (MFN) tariff (HTS 8703) would be 2.5% and for South Korea it would be 8%.

[51] The truck tariff applies to "motor vehicles for the transport of goods (HTS 8704)" which would include trucks like the Ford F-150.

[52] Displacement is one measurement of car engines. An engine in cubic centimeters shows the volumes displaced by the cylinders through one revolution. Typically, a higher number means a more powerful engine. Engine displacement can also be measured in liters (e.g., a 1.4 liter engine is equivalent to 1,400 cc and a 1.8 liter engine is equivalent to 1,800 cc). A small car engine is generally around 1.6 liter such as the Hyundai Elantra; examples of larger engines include the Ford Fusion at 2.5 liters and the Chevy Impala with an engine as large as 5.3 liters.

[53] The 2007 agreement allowed no more than 6,500 vehicles per year per U.S. automotive manufacturer.

[54] South Korea's new environmental regulations will become more stringent over the next five years. These new regulations, which are still being developed, took effect in 2012 and are expected to remain in place until 2015. South Korea will raise the average fuel economy of automobiles seating 10 or fewer passengers to 17 kilometers per liter and will lower the standard for carbon dioxide emissions to 140 grams per kilometer by 2015. Automobile importers would be able to choose either standard to satisfy the requirement.

[55] USTR. *Agreed Minutes*, February 10, 2011, http://www.ustr.gov/webfm_send/2555.

[56] A list of KORUS Committees and Working Groups can be found at http://www.ustr.gov /countries-regions/japankorea-apec/korea/korus-committees-and-working-groups.

[57] White House. "*Increasing U.S. Auto Exports and Growing U.S. Auto Jobs Through the U.S.-Korea Trade Agreement*," December 3, 2010, http://www.whitehouse.gov/sites/default /files/ fact_sheet_increasing_us_auto_exports_us_ korea_free_trade_agreement.pdf.

[58] Bryan Laviolette, *GM Daewoo Changing Name to GM Korea*, Detr oit News, January 20, 2011.

[59] Ibid. *U.S.-Korea FTA*, Table 2.2.

[60] Ibid. *U.S.-Korea FTA*, p. 3-78.

[61] Ibid. *U.S.-Korea FTA.*

[62] Energy Efficiency and Renewable Energy, U.S. Department of Energy, *Alternative Fuels & Advanced Vehicles Data Center*, HEV Sales by Model, 1999-2011, http://www.afdc.energy. gov/data/tab/vehicles/data_set/10301.

[63] Mark Williams, *"Hyundai Says No, But Kia Could Say Yes,"* PickupTrucks.com, February, 20, 2012, http://news.pickuptrucks.com/2012/02/hyundai-says-no-but-kia-could-say-yes.html.

[64] According to *WardsAuto*, Hyundai produced 113,000 "Porters," and Kia produced 87,000 "Bongos," both described as pickups in 2012.

[65] Textile and apparel statistics are compiled from the Office of Textiles and Apparel (OTEXA) U.S, textiles and apparel trade balance report. Textiles comprise yarn, fabric, and made-up articles (e.g., sheets and towels), http://otexa.ita.doc.gov/.

[66] United States International Trade Commission. *U.S.-Korea Free Trade Agreement: Potential Economy-Wide and Selected Sectoral Effects.* USITC Publication 3949. September 2007. pp. 3-52.

[67] World Trade Organization. *Tariff Profiles for South Korea and the United States*, 2012, http://www.wto.org/english/res_e/booksp_e/tariff_profiles12_e.pdf.

[68] USITC. pp. 3-52.

[69] OTEXA, South Korea, Market Reports, Textiles, Apparel, Footwear, and Travel Goods, http://web.ita.doc.gov/tacgi/overseasnew.nsf/country/Korea-South.

[70] Ibid. *U.S.-Korea FTA*, pp. 3-53.

[71] Ibid., *U.S.-Korea FTA* , Table 2.2.

[72] Ibid., pp. 3-68 and 3-71.

[73] Aerospace products and parts are classified under North American Industry Classification System (NAICS) code 3364. Data compiled from the International Trade Commission, Interactive Tariff and Trade Dataweb, (accessed March 1, 2013).

[74] U.S. Commercial Service, *Doing Business in Korea: 2012 Country Commercial Guide for U.S. Companies*, p. 25, 2012.

[75] Computers and electronic products are classified under NAICS 334 and semiconductors and other electronic components under NAICS 3344. Data compiled from the International Trade Commission, Interactive Tariff and Trade Dataweb, (accessed March 1, 2013).

[76] Ibid., *U.S.-Korea FTA* , pp. 3-68 through 3-73.

[77] Steel products include all iron and steel items listed with the two digit Harmonized Tariff Schedule (HTS) codes 72 and 73.

[78] USITC. p. 3-64.

[79] Ibid. p. 3-91.

[80] The pharmaceuticals and medicines statistics are based on NAICS 3254 and medical equipment and supplies NAICS 3391 were compiled using the International Trade Administration's Trade Stats Express, http://tse.export.gov/TSE/ TSEhome.aspx

[81] *WorldTrade Online,* March 16, 2012.

[82] Primosch, William. *Testimony of Senior Director, International Business Policy, National Association of Manufacturers on the Proposed United States-Korea Free Trade Agreement for the Trade Policy Staff Committee, Office of the U.S. Trade Representative.* March 14, 2006. p. 6.

[83] Report of the United States Industry Trade Advisory Committee for Chemicals, Pharmaceuticals, Health/Science Products, and Service (ITAC-3) on The United States-South Korea Trade Promotion Agreement. April 24, 2007.

[84] International Trade Administration, *Pharmaceuticals Industry Profile 2010*, p. 8, July 2010.

[85] Economist Intelligence Unit, *South Korea: Healthcare and Pharmaceuticals Report*, Industry Briefing, August 23, 2012.

[86] Jeong-Seok Lee, Industrial and Regulatory Perspectives on Pharmaceuticals in Korea, p. 6, November 2011.

[87] U.S. Commercial Service, *Doing Business In Korea: 2012 Country Commercial Guide for U.S. Companies*, pp. 46-8, 2012.

[88] USITC. *U.S.-Korea FTA*, p. 3-91.

[89] Pharmaceuticals are classified under NAICS 3254 and medical equipment and supplies under NAICS 3391. Data compiled from the International Trade Commission, Interactive Tariff and Trade Dataweb, (accessed March 1, 2013).

[90] Primosch, William. *Testimony of Senior Director, International Business Policy, National Association of Manufacturers on the Proposed United States-Korea Free Trade Agreement for the Trade Policy Staff Committee, Office of the U.S. Trade Representative.* March 14, 2006. p. 6.

[91] Data obtained from U.S. Department of Commerce. Bureau of Economic Analysis.

[92] Ibid.

[93] USITC. p. 4-8.

[94] Office of the United States Trade Representative. *2007 National Trade Estimates Report—Foreign Trade Barriers*. p. 366.

[95] The United States-Korea Free Trade Agreement (KORUS FTA). Report of the Industry Trade Advisory Committee on Services and Finance Industries (ITAC 10) April 2007.

[96] The Free Trade Agreement Between South Korea and the United States (KORUS FTA). Chapter 13 (Financial Services)—Confirming Letter.

[97] Annex -I (Korea).

[98] KORUS FTA Chapter 14 Telecommunications.

[99] Coalition of Service Industries. *Coalition of Service Industries Expresses Strong Support for U.S.-Korea FTA; Urges Swift Congressional Passage.* Press release. June 30, 2007.

[100] White House Office of the Press Secretary, "President Bush Discusses the Visa Waiver Program," October 17, 2008. South Korea's path to entry into the VWP was made possible by reforms of the VWP that were embodied in H.R. 1 (P.L. 110-53), the Implementing the 9/11 Commission Recommendations Act of 2007. For more on the U.S. Visa Waiver Program, see CRS Report RL32221, *Visa Waiver Program*, by Alison Siskin.

[101] Department of Homeland Security, Temporary Admissions in *Yearbook of Immigration Statistics: 2007* Table 28.

[102] *Inside U.S. Trade*, December 10, 2010.

[103] This section on trade remedies was written by Vivian C. Jones, Specialist in International Trade and Finance, Foreign Affairs, Defense, and Trade Division, CRS.

[104] For more information, see CRS Report RL32371, *Trade Remedies: A Primer*, by Vivian C. Jones.

[105] P.L. 107-210, Trade Act of 2002, §2102(b)(14).

[106] "South Korea Retracts Key Demand in Anti-Dumping Rules: Leaked Government Report," *Yonhap* (South Korea), January 19, 2007.

[107] USITC. "Antidumping and Countervailing Duty Orders In Place As of September 10, 2008, by Country." Available at http://www.usitc.gov. Korea Trade Commission, TR Measures, available at http://www.ktc.go.kr/en/kboard_child/ list.jsp?bm=86&pg=1.

[108] Schott, Jeffrey J., Bradford, Scott C., and Moll, Thomas. *Negotiating the Korea - United States Free Trade Agreement*, Institute for International Economics, June 2006.

[109] World Trade Organization dispute settlement statistics, http://www.wto.org/english /tratop_e/dispu_e/ dispu_by_country_e.htm. South Korea was one of the complainants in the WTO dispute brought against the U.S. safeguard measures on steel, as well as that against the Continued Dumping and Subsidy Offset Act ("Byrd Amendment").

[110] "Cutler says U.S.-Korea Talks Hit Snag in Three Negotiating Groups, *FDA Week*, December 8, 2006. Although the particulars of South Korean demands were not made public, according to news reports, one of Korea's demands was to be excluded from the cumulation of imports used to determine injury in a safeguards case, if its share of imports into the U.S. are below a certain threshold.

[111] "South Korea Retracts Key Demand on Anti-dumping Rules: Leaked Government Report." *Yonhap*, January 19, 2007.

[112] See Chapter 10, §A, Article 10.1 Application of a Safeguard Measure and Article 10.5 Global Safeguard Actions.

[113] Article 10.4, Compensation.

[114] Chapter 10, §B. Antidumping and Countervailing.

[115] CVD: 19 U.S.C. 1671c; AD: 19 U.S.C. 1673c. Under these statutes, a quantitative restriction or price offset suspension agreement must completely eliminate the injurious effect of the dumping or subsidy, must be in the public interest and must be able to be effectively monitored by U.S. authorities.

[116] Chapter 10, §B. Antidumping and Countervailing Duties, Article 10.7, paragraphs 3 and 4.

[117] Chapter 10, §C. Committee on Trade Remedies, Article 10.8, paragraph 2.

[118] ITAC (12) on Steel, Advisory Committee Report, April 27, 2007, p. 7.

[119] Ibid., p. 4

[120] Ibid.

[121] "Trade Remedy Piece of Korea FTA Ignores Korean AD Demands," *Inside U.S. Trade*, April 13, 2007.

[122] Ibid.

[123] For more, see CRS Report RL34093, *The Kaesong North-South Korean Industrial Complex*, by Mark E. Manyin and Dick K. Nanto.

[124] In July 2011, South Korea's largest opposition party, the Democratic Party, called for the KORUS FTA to be rewritten to recognize KIC-made products as South Korean in origin.

[125] Chapter 22, Annex B, Committee on Outward Processing Zones on the Korean Peninsula.

[126] April 2007 interviews with U.S. and Korean officials; remarks by Assistant U.S. Trade Representative for Japan, Korea and APEC Affairs Wendy Cutler at an April 5, 2007, Korea Economic Institute forum; "Behind the Korea FTA Negotiations," *Washington Trade Daily*, April 12, 2007.

[127] March 2011 document issued by the Office Of The United States Trade Representative, "Outward Processing Zones, Kaesong, and the U.S.-Korea Trade Agreement Frequently Asked Questions"; Deputy United States Trade Representative reiterated this point in April 7, 2011, testimony before the House Ways and Means Trade Subcommittee.

[128] CRS calculations based on data from U.S. Department of Commerce. Bureau of Economic Analysis, at http://www.bea.gov.

[129] A range of factors determine the climate for foreign investment—government regulations, skills of local labor, general economic conditions, intellectual property rights protection, among others. Therefore, U.S.-South Korean investment ties could be affected by not only the provisions of the investment chapter of the agreement, but other chapters as well.

[130] The USITC report on the KORUS FTA points out that South Korea's list these "nonconforming measures" in the KORUS FTA is longer than in previous FTAs that the United States has signed; however, industry representatives generally believe that the KORUS FTA would still render significant opportunities for U.S. investors. USITC. p. 6-5.

[131] USITC. p. 6-5.

[132] A national treatment exception is made with respect to the secondary uses of recordings by means of analog communications, including over-the-air broadcasts, whereby a Party can limit the rights of performers and producers of sound recordings from the other Party on its own territory. This exception was a disappointment to U.S. industry, which otherwise praise the agreement. *Korea-U.S. Free Trade Agreement: Benefits to America's Entertainment Industries.* Testimony Before the U.S. International Trade Commission by Greg Frazier, Executive Vice-President Worldwide Government Policy Motion Picture Association of America. June 6, 2007. p.7.

[133] The FTA would require each Party to adopt and maintain five internationally accepted labor rights that are contained in the ILO Declaration on Fundamental Principles and Rights at Work and Its Follow-Up (1998) (ILO Declaration) Article 19:2 specifies these rights as the freedom of association, the effective recognition of the right to collective bargaining, the

elimination of all forms of compulsory or forced labor, the effective abolition of child labor and the elimination of discrimination in respect of employment and occupation. The framework also requires FTAs to adhere to seven major multilateral environmental agreements and for this commitment to be enforceable under the FTA. "The Trade Policy for America" was completed after President Bush notified Congress on April 1, 2007, of his intention to sign the KORUS FTA but prior to the signing on June 30. At first, South Korean officials balked at opening negotiations to add the language but eventually agreed to do so. After, the two sides held negotiations, they included the language in the final text that was signed on June 30, 2007.

[134] In Questions for the Record posed by members of the Senate Finance Committee, USTR Kirk was asked "Do you think that the labor and environment provisions of the U.S.-Korea FTA are appropriate?" He responded that "the U.S.- Korea FTA incorporates the May 10th Agreement, which established a strong foundation for bipartisan progress on trade." United States Senate Committee on Finance, "Finance Committee Questions For The Record. Hearing on Confirmation of Mr. Ronald Kirk to be United States Trade Representative," March 9, 2009.

[135] OECD, *Economic Survey—Korea 2007*, p. 138.

[136] Report of the Labor Advisory Committee for Trade Negotiations and Trade Policy (LAC) on the KORUS FTA, April 27, 2007, p. 9.

[137] *Ibid.*

[138] OECD, *Economic Survey—Korea 2007*, pp. 128-40.

[139] The seven agreements are: the Convention on International Trade in Endangered Species; the Montreal Protocol on Ozone Depleting Substances; the Convention on Marine Pollution; the Inter-American Tropical Tuna Convention; the Ramsar Convention on the Wetlands; the International Convention for the Regulation of Whaling; and the Convention on Conservation of Antarctic Marine Living Resources.

[140] United States Senate Committee on Finance, "Finance Committee Questions For The Record. Hearing on Confirmation of Mr. Ronald Kirk to be United States Trade Representative," March 9, 2009.

[141] Reportedly, the GNP took this step after learning that the DP and its allies were planning to occupy the National Assembly's main chamber in order to block a vote on the KORUS FTA.

[142] Korea Broadcast System, March 31, 2006, Broadcast in Korean, summarized by the Open Source Center, "ROK TV Carries Economic Minister's Comments on ROK-US FTA," April 10, 2006, FEA20060410021900. (Han was Finance Minister when he made these remarks.) South Korean Blue House, "Address to the Nation," April 2, 2007.

[143] EFTA is comprised of Iceland, Norway, Switzerland, and Liechtenstein. The 10-member ASEAN consists of Brunei, Cambodia, Indonesia, Laos, Malaysia, Myanmar, Philippines, Singapore, Thailand, and Vietnam.

[144] For more, see CRS Report R41481, *U.S.-South Korea Relations*, coordinated by Mark E. Manyin.

[145] Andrew Green, "South Korea's Automobile Industry: Development and Prospects," *Asian Survey*, vol. 32, no. 5 (May 1992), pp. 413-414.

[146] International Organization of Motor Vehicle Manufacturers (OICA), *World Motor Vehicle Production*, World Ranking of Manufacturers, 2011 Production Statistics, http://oica.net/category/production-statistics/.

[147] American Automotive Policy Council, "*Statistical Overview of the Korean Automotive Industry/Market & U.S. Trade Relationship, 1990-2012*," http://www.americanautocouncil.org/industry-facts.

[148] USITC. *Industry and Trade Summary: Motor Vehicles* (USITC Publication 3545, September 2002), p. 60.

[149] Ibid., pp. 60-61; Graeme P. Maxton and John Wormald, *Time for a Model Change: Re-Engineering the Global Automotive Industry.* Cambridge, U.K.: Cambridge University Press, 2004. pp. 101-2; CRS Report RL32883, *U.S. Automotive Industry: Recent History and Issues*, by Stephen Cooney and Brent D. Yacobucci, pp. 75-76.

[150] OICA, *World Motor Vehicle Production*, World Ranking of Manufacturers, Year 2011, http://oica.net/wpcontent/uploads/ranking-without-china-30-nov-12.pdf.

[151] American Automotive Policy Council, "*Statistical Overview of the Korean Automotive Industry/Market & U.S. Trade Relationship, 1990-2012*," http://www.americanautocouncil.org/industry-facts

[152] "*U.S. Light Vehicle Sales, December & YTD*," WardsAuto, January 4, 2013, http://www.wardsauto.com and data from the American Automotive Policy Council.

[153] "*North American Production by Vehicle Line*," WardsAuto, January 10, 2013, http://wardsauto.com.

[154] American Automotive Policy Council, *Facts about the Korean Auto Industry and Economy*, http://www.americanautocouncil.org/.

[155] Ibid.

[156] Sang-yirl Nam, "Implications of Liberalizing Korea-U.S. Trade in the Automobile Sector: Potential Impact of the Korea-U.S. Free Trade Agreement," Korea Economic Institute *Academic Paper Series*, III:1 (February 2008), p. 10.

[157] "*U.S. Light Vehicle Sales,*" WardsAuto, January 4, 2013, http://www.wardsauto.com and data from the American Automotive Policy Council.

[158] CRS Report RL32883, *U.S. Automotive Industry: Recent History and Issues*, by Stephen Cooney and Brent D. Yacobucci, p. 60.

[159] To complete the picture, General Motors has sold over 100,000 cars annually since 2005 through its South Korean subsidiary, the GM Korea operations. The rest of its production, which totaled nearly 882,000 vehicles, were shipped abroad. General Motors Corporation and Korea's Daewoo Motor Company launched the GM Daewoo Auto & Technology Company in 2002, renamed GM Korea in 2011. GM holds a 72% stake in the Korean car maker, with the rest of the company controlled by the state run Korea Development Bank. GM Daewoo operates five manufacturing facilities in Korea and one assembly plant in Vietnam.

INDEX

C

D

E

F

G

H

I

N

O

P

Q

R

S

T

U

V

W

Y